Kotlin for Android Developers

Learn Kotlin the easy way while developing an Android App

Antonio Leiva

D1731546

Kotlin for Android Developers

Learn Kotlin the easy way while developing an Android App

Antonio Leiva

ISBN 978-1530075614

Leanpub

This is a Leanpub book. Leanpub empowers authors and publishers with the Lean Publishing process. Lean Publishing is the act of publishing an in-progress ebook using lightweight tools and many iterations to get reader feedback, pivot until you have the right book and build traction once you do.

This book is dedicated to all the loyal readers of antonioleiva.com, who made me believe that writing about Android development was a powerful tool to help others learn about it. I felt that this book was a necessary step forward.

Special mention goes to Luis Herrero, who designed the excellent cover of this book, and to Gautier Mechling for helping me so much by reviewing this book. It is thanks to him that these pages are not full of typos and mistakes.

And, of course, this is specially dedicated to you. With your support and your help, this book is growing and becoming a reference. So any suggestions to improve the quality of this book will be welcomed. Feel free to write anytime to contact@antonioleiva.com.

Contents

I. About this book

Hey! Thanks so much for your interest in this book, I am thrilled that you decided to become a Kotlin for Android expert.

Many things have happened since I started writing "Kotlin for Android Developers" in mid-2015. At that point, Kotlin was still in an early access edition. However, I felt so much power in the language, that I decided to explain everything that I was learning in a book.

Since then, the language has kept growing to the point that Google announced that they would start supporting Kotlin as an official language to develop Android apps.

These were amazing news. But it was even more amazing that both Google and JetBrains suggested this book to Android developers who want to learn the language.

As you may know, this is a lean publication. This book grew and progressed thanks to the readers' comments. So I can only thank you for helping me bring this dream to life.

What is "Kotlin for Android Developers" about

Throughout this book, I create an Android app from the ground up using Kotlin as the primary language. The idea is to learn the language by example, instead of following a regular reference book structure. I will be stopping to explain the most useful concepts and ideas about Kotlin, comparing them to Java 6. This way, you can see what the differences are and which parts of the language can help you speed up your work.

This book is not meant to be a language reference, but a tool for Android developers to learn Kotlin and be able to continue with their projects by themselves. The examples are meant to overcome the most recurring problems we have to face in our daily lives as app developers, by making use of Kotlin's expressiveness and some other exciting tools and libraries. However, this text covers most of the features of Kotlin, so by the end of the reading, you will have an in-depth knowledge of the language.

The content is very practical, so I recommend that you follow the examples and the code in front of a computer and try everything it suggests. You could, however, take one first read to get a broad idea and then dive into practice.

Even though this book now finished, I will review it from time to time to keep it up to date with new Kotlin versions. So feel free to write and tell me what you think about the book, or what could be improved. I want this book to be the perfect tool for Android developers, and as such, help and ideas will be welcomed.

If you are reading a printed copy and want to receive the latest updates, please feel free to email me at *contact@antonioleiva.com* with a proof of purchase, and I will give you access to the digital copy. That way, you will keep receiving the updates. Do the same if you got it from any bookstores (Kindle, Kobo…) and you want to get access to the PDF version.

Thanks for becoming part of this exciting project!

II. Is this book for you?

This book is written to be useful to Android developers who are interested in learning the Kotlin language.

This book is for you if you are in some of the following situations:

- You have some basic knowledge of Android Development and the Android SDK, as well as the Java language.
- You want to learn how to develop Android apps using Kotlin by following an example.
- You need a guide on how to solve many of the common challenges Android developers face every day, by using a cleaner and more expressive language.

On the other hand, this book may not be for you. These are the topics that you will not find in it:

- The content of these pages is not a Kotlin Bible. I shall explain all language basics, and even more complicated ideas when they come out during the process, just when we need them. So you will learn by example and not the other way round.
- I will not explain how to develop an Android app. You do not need a deep understanding of the platform, but at least some basics, such as some knowledge of Android Studio, Gradle, Java programming and Android SDK. You may even learn some new Android things in the process!
- The book is not a guide to functional programming. Of course, I am showing what you need, as Java 6 is not functional at all, but I will not dive deep into the programming paradigm.

III. About the author

Hi! This is Antonio Leiva.

Since the end of 2018, I am self-employed. I spend my time helping Android developers and the companies they work for to transition from Java to Kotlin. By mastering the language, they manage to boost their productivity and create more robust and maintainable software.

I am really thankful for having had the opportunity to help thousands of people with my content, which goes from my regular posts in my blog antonioleiva.com to this book you currently have in your hands.

I also became a **Kotlin Certified Training by JetBrains**, so I am proud to offer certified training, which you or your company can participate in. I have both online and live training. If you are interested in any of them, please write me to contact@antonioleiva.com[1]. As a valued customer, I can offer you huge discounts on the online training[2].

If you want to know a little about me, I live in Madrid, Spain. I've been working as a software developer for more than 10 years. I started as a CRM consultant, but at some point, I found Android and quickly fell in love. Since that, I moved from my first company to another one called Gigigo, a Spanish brand that built third-party Apps.

Finally, I had the chance to join Plex[3] and start working remotely. It was a vast and challenging experience as an Android developer that helped me learn a lot of how a software company works.

But in the meanwhile, the success of this book made me realize that there was a considerable need wanting to be covered, so I started running my own business. When our baby was born, my spare time was highly reduced, so I had to make a

---

[1]mailto:contact@antonioleiva.com
[2]https://antonioleiva.com/online-course/
[3]https://plex.tv

decision. That led me to focus 100% on helping other Android developers boost their careers.

On my free time, I just like enjoying all the little moments I can with my family. I also love cooking, especially since I became vegan and had to reinvent the way I eat every day. And of course, I enjoy new technologies and staying up to date as much as I can in this sector.

If you want to keep in contact and know more about my day-to-day, you can follow me on my different places:

- Blog: antonioleiva.com[4]
- Twitter: @lime_cl[5]
- Instagram: antonioleivag[6]
- Facebook Group: Kotlin for Android Developers[7]
- YouTube Channel: Tutorials & Interviews[8]
- LinkedIn: antoniolg[9]

I hope you enjoy this book!

---

[4]http://antonioleiva.com
[5]https://twitter.com/lime_cl
[6]https://www.instagram.com/antonioleivag/
[7]https://www.facebook.com/groups/kotlinandroiddev/
[8]https://www.youtube.com/c/antonioleivacom
[9]https://www.linkedin.com/in/antoniolg/

1 Introduction

Things are changing for good for Android Developers. In Google I/O 2017, the Android team announced that Kotlin was becoming an official language to develop Android apps.

This means that, while it is still possible to develop Android apps using Java, from now on Kotlin is fully supported, and Google is making sure that every new Android feature, the framework, the IDE and all their libraries work seamlessly with the new language.

Google listened to the community, who was asking for years that Kotlin became a first-party language. So you can now take advantage of all the features of a modern language while developing for Android.

Throughout this book, I will show you how, so I hope that I can help you understand the various ways that Kotlin can take you one step ahead and make your code much better.

However, before diving into the features of the language, let me tell you just a little bit of background.

1.1 What is Kotlin?

Kotlin is language developed by JetBrains[10], a company known for building the IntelliJ IDEA, a powerful IDE for Java development. Android Studio, the official Android IDE, is based on IntelliJ. It was initially implemented to run on the Java Virtual Machine.

JetBrains designed Kotlin with Java developers in mind, and with IntelliJ as its primary development IDE. These two factors are breaking points that made Android developers quickly adopt the language:

---

[10]https://www.jetbrains.com/

- **Kotlin is very intuitive and easy to learn for Java developers**. Most parts of the language are very similar to what we already know, and the differences can be mastered in no time.
- **We have total integration with our daily IDE for free**. Android Studio can understand, compile and run Kotlin code. Moreover, the support for this language comes from the company who develops the IDE, so we Android developers are first-class citizens.

However, this is only related to how the language integrates with our tools. What are the advantages of the language when compared to Java 6?

- ** It is more expressive**: this is one of its main points. You can write more with much less code.
- ** It is safer**: Kotlin is null safe, which means that we deal with possible null situations at compile time, to prevent execution time exceptions. We need to specify that an object can be null explicitly, and then check its nullity before using it. You can save much time debugging null pointer exceptions and fixing nullity bugs.
- ** It is functional**: Kotlin is fundamentally an object-oriented language, not a pure functional language. However, like many other modern languages, it uses many concepts from functional programming, such as lambda expressions, to solve some problems more naturally. Another nice feature is the way it deals with collections.
- **It makes use of extension functions**: This means we can extend any class with new features even if we do not have access to the source code.
- ** It is highly interoperable**: You can continue using most libraries and code written in Java because the interoperability between both languages is excellent. It is even possible to create mixed projects, with both Kotlin and Java files coexisting.

However, this is only the tip of the iceberg: - Since Kotlin 1.1, the final version of Kotlin JS[11] was released. This new variant allows you to develop web apps using Kotlin. - Since Kotlin 1.2, you can also create multiplatform projects[12]. With it, you

---

[11]https://kotlinlang.org/docs/reference/js-overview.html
[12]https://kotlinlang.org/docs/reference/whatsnew12.html#multiplatform-projects-experimental

can share code between JVM and Javascript. - The JetBrains team has also released Kotlin/Native[13], a project that finally takes Kotlin out of the JVM. Thanks to it, you will be able to implement the server, the web and the Android and iOS Apps using Kotlin for most of the code base. - Gradle 5.0 has added support to Kotlin DSL (a simplified version of Kotlin) to write Gradle files instead of Groovy. This is already an official feature that you can start using today. You can read more in Gradle's blog[14].

So you can see that the future of Kotlin is pretty promising. Learning Kotlin can become the language of reference in many other platforms, and sharing code among all them is undoubtedly a high selling point.

1.2 What do we get with Kotlin?

Without diving too deep into the Kotlin language (we will learn everything about it throughout this book), these are some interesting features we miss in Java:

Expressiveness

With Kotlin, it is much easier to avoid boilerplate because the language covers the most common patterns by default. For instance, in Java, if we want to create a data class, we need to write (or at least generate) this code:

```
1   public class Artist {
2       private long id;
3       private String name;
4       private String url;
5       private String mbid;
6
7       public long getId() {
8           return id;
9       }
10
11      public void setId(long id) {
12          this.id = id;
```

---

[13]https://kotlinlang.org/docs/reference/native-overview.html
[14]https://blog.gradle.org/kotlin-dsl-1.0

```
13        }
14
15        public String getName() {
16            return name;
17        }
18
19        public void setName(String name) {
20            this.name = name;
21        }
22
23        public String getUrl() {
24            return url;
25        }
26
27        public void setUrl(String url) {
28            this.url = url;
29        }
30
31        public String getMbid() {
32            return mbid;
33        }
34
35        public void setMbid(String mbid) {
36            this.mbid = mbid;
37        }
38
39        @Override public String toString() {
40            return "Artist{" +
41                    "id=" + id +
42                    ", name='" + name + '\'' +
43                    ", url='" + url + '\'' +
44                    ", mbid='" + mbid + '\'' +
45                    '}';
46        }
47    }
```

With Kotlin, you just need to make use of a data class:

```
1   data class Artist(
2       var id: Long,
3       var name: String,
4       var url: String,
5       var mbid: String)
```

This data class auto-generates all the fields and property accessors, as well as some useful methods such as toString(). You also get equals() and hashCode() for free, which are very verbose and can be dangerous if they are incorrectly implemented.

Null Safety

When we use Java, a significant amount of our code is defensive. We need to check once and another whether something is null before using it to prevent unexpected *NullPointerException*. Kotlin, like many other modern languages, is null-safe because the type explicitly defines whether an object can be null by using the safe call operator (written ?).

We can do things like this:

```
1   // This does not compile. Artist cannot be null
2   var notNullArtist: Artist = null
3
4   // Artist can be null
5   var artist: Artist? = null
6
7   // Will not compile, artist could be null and we need to deal with that
8   artist.print()
9
10  // Will print only if artist != null
11  artist?.print()
12
13  // Smart cast. We don not need to use safe call operator if we previously
14  // checked nullity
15  if (artist != null) {
16      artist.print()
17  }
18
19  // Only use it when we are sure it is not null. It throws an exception otherwise.
20  artist!!.print()
21
```

```
22    // Use Elvis operator to give an alternative in case the object is null.
23    val name = artist?.name ?: "empty"
```

Extension functions

Thanks to extension functions, you can add new functions to any class. It is a cleaner substitute for the common utility classes we all have in our projects. You could, for instance, add a new method to fragments to show a toast:

```
1    fun Fragment.toast(message: CharSequence, duration: Int = Toast.LENGTH_SHORT) {
2        Toast.makeText(getActivity(), message, duration).show()
3    }
```

And then use it like this:

```
1    fragment.toast("Hello world!")
```

Functional support (Lambdas)

What if, instead of having to declare an anonymous class every time we need to implement a click listener, we could just define what we want to do? We can indeed do it. This (and many other interesting things) is what we get thanks to lambdas:

```
1    view.setOnClickListener { toast("Hello world!") }
```

This set of features is only a small selection of what Kotlin can do to simplify your code. Now that you know some of the many great features of the language, you may decide that this is not for you. If you continue, we will start writing some code right away in the next chapter.

2 Getting ready

Now that you know some little examples of what you may do with Kotlin, I am sure you want to start to put it into practice as soon as possible. Don't worry; these first chapters will help you configure your development environment so that you can start writing some code immediately.

2.1 Android Studio

The first thing you need is to install Android Studio. As you may know, Android Studio is the official Android IDE, which was presented to the public in 2013 as a preview and finally released in 2014.

Android Studio is implemented as a plugin for IntelliJ IDEA[15], a Java IDE created by Jetbrains[16], the company which is also behind Kotlin. So, as you can see, everything is tightly connected.

The adoption of Android Studio was a significant step forward for Android developers. First, because we left the buggy Eclipse behind and moved to a set of tools specially designed for Java developers, which gives us a whole interaction with the language. We enjoy fantastic features such as fast and impressively smart code completion, and powerful analyzing and refactoring tools among others.

And second, Gradle[17] became the official build system for Android, which means a whole bunch of new possibilities relating to versioning, building, and deployment. Two of the most exciting functions are build types and flavors, which let you create infinite versions of the app (or even different apps) in a straightforward way while using the same code base.

If you are still using Eclipse, I am afraid you need to switch to Android Studio if you want to follow this book. The Kotlin team is creating a plugin for Eclipse, but it

[15]https://www.jetbrains.com/idea
[16]https://www.jetbrains.com
[17]https://gradle.org/

may be far behind the one for Android Studio, and the integration is probably less smooth. You will also discover what you are missing as soon you start using it.

I am not covering the use of Android Studio or Gradle because this is not the focus of the book. But if this is the first time you use these tools, I am sure that you will be able to follow the content and learn the basics in the meanwhile.

Download Android Studio from the official page[18] if you do not have it already.

2.2 Install Kotlin plugin

Since IntelliJ 15 was released, the Kotlin plugin is bundled with the IDE. For Android Studio, it depends on the version you are using.

If you have Android Studio 3.0 or above, you already have everything you need. If your Android Studio is 2.3 or below, you need to install the Kotlin plugin manually.

So go to the plugins section inside *Android Studio Preferences*, and install the Kotlin plugin. Use the search tool if you cannot find it.

Now our environment is ready to understand the language, compile it and execute it just as seamlessly as if we were using Java.

---

[18]https://developer.android.com/sdk/index.html

3 Creating a new project

So now it is time to start creating our App. I want to keep the explanation simple on purpose, because Android Studio wizard changes from time to time and these lines can become deprecated pretty soon.

Our app consists of a simple weather app, such as the one used in Google's Beginners Course from Udacity[19]. We will be paying attention to different things, but the idea of the app is the same because it includes many of the things you find in a regular app. If you are starting with Android development, I recommend you this course.

3.1 Create a new project in Android Studio

Again, there is a small difference depending on the Android Studio version you are using.

For Android Studio 3, the steps are pretty straightforward. Previous versions require a little more work, but it is far from complicated too. Even if you are already using new versions of Android Studio, I recommend you to take a look to the whole process, because it is what you would need to do if you want to start using Kotlin on a Java project.

First of all, open Android Studio and choose `Create New Project`. The first step is to decide a name for your app; you can use the name you want: `WeatherApp` for instance. Then the wizard asks for a Company Domain. As you are not releasing the app, this field is not very important either, but if you own a domain, you can use that one. Also, choose the location where you want to save the project.

In Android Studio 3, at this point, you find a checkbox that enables Kotlin support. So select it if that is your case.

For the next step, the wizard asks for the minimum API version. I selected API 15 for the sample app, but Kotlin does not have any restrictions regarding the minimum API. Skip any other platform different to `Phone and Tablet` for now.

---

[19]https://udacity.com/course/new-android-fundamentals--ud851

Finally, we are required to choose an activity template. Select `Empty Activity`. This template generates little code, and it is easier for us to add new logic.

Keep the name of the activities or layouts in the next screen. We will change them later if we need to. Press `Finish` and let Android Studio do its work.

With Android Studio 3 you are done, skip to point 3.4. The next two steps are only required if you had to install the plugin manually.

3.2 Convert MainActivity to Kotlin code

An interesting feature that the Kotlin plugin includes is the ability to convert from Java to Kotlin code. As an automated process, it is not perfect, but it may help a lot during your first days until you start getting used to the Kotlin language.

So we are using this in our `MainActivity.java` class. Open the file and select `Code -> Convert Java File to Kotlin File`. Take a look at the differences, so that you start becoming familiar with the language.

You can also copy any Java code into a Kotlin file, and the plugin also converts it.

3.3 Configure Kotlin in project

The Kotlin plugin also includes a tool that configures the Gradle files for us.

Just go to `Tools -> Project -> Configure Kotlin in Project`. Choose the latest Kotlin version, and press OK.

Review the changes. There should be something like this:

build.gradle

```
1   buildscript {
2       ext.kotlin_version = '1.3.20'
3       repositories {
4           jcenter()
5       }
6       dependencies {
7           classpath 'com.android.tools.build:gradle:3.3.0'
8           classpath "org.jetbrains.kotlin:kotlin-gradle-plugin:$kotlin_version"
9       }
10  }
11
12  allprojects {
13      repositories {
14          jcenter()
15      }
16  }
```

As you can see, it is creating a variable that saves the current Kotlin version. We need that version number in several places, for instance in the new dependency to the Kotlin plugin.

It will be useful again in the module `build.gradle`, where the configuration has also added a dependency to the **Kotlin standard library**. Go check it now:

app/build.gradle

```
1   apply plugin: 'com.android.application'
2   apply plugin: 'kotlin-android'
3
4   android {
5       ...
6   }
7
8   dependencies {
9       implementation "org.jetbrains.kotlin:kotlin-stdlib:$kotlin_version"
10  }
```

3.4 Include some other useful configuration

There are some other extra libraries that we will be using, so take the chance to add them to the build.gradle.

An important one is Anko, a library that uses the power of Kotlin to simplify some tasks in Android. We will use more modules of Anko later on, but for now, it is enough to add anko-common. This library is split into several smaller ones so that we include in the project only the parts we require.

Let's go to the main one first, and update the buildscript by adding two new variables for the support libraries as well as Anko library (you can also check the latest version here[20]). This way, it is easier to modify all the versions in a row, as well as adding new libraries that use the same version without having to change it everywhere:

build.gradle

```
1  buildscript {
2      ext.support_version = '28.0.0'
3      ext.kotlin_version = '1.3.20'
4      ext.anko_version = '0.10.8'
5      repositories {
6          jcenter()
7          google()
8      }
9      dependencies {
10         classpath 'com.android.tools.build:gradle:3.3.0'
11         classpath "org.jetbrains.kotlin:kotlin-gradle-plugin:$kotlin_version"
12     }
13 }
14
15 allprojects {
16     repositories {
17         jcenter()
18         google()
19     }
20 }
```

If you are using Android Studio 2.3, you also need to add the Google repository as you can see above. Android Studio 3 does it for you.

---

[20]https://github.com/Kotlin/anko/releases

Let's then add the **Anko** library dependency to the module file, update the **AppCompat** to use our variable, and apply the **Kotlin Android Extensions** plugin:

app/build.gradle

```
1   apply plugin: 'com.android.application'
2   apply plugin: 'kotlin-android'
3   apply plugin: 'kotlin-android-extensions'
4
5   android {
6       ...
7   }
8
9   dependencies {
10      implementation "com.android.support:appcompat-v7:$support_version"
11      implementation "org.jetbrains.kotlin:kotlin-stdlib:$kotlin_version"
12      implementation "org.jetbrains.anko:anko-common:$anko_version"
13  }
```

With these changes, we should be ready to start.

3.5 Test that everything works

We are going to add some code to check that Kotlin Android Extensions are fully functional. I am not explaining much about it yet, but I want to be sure this is working for you.

First, go to `activity_main.xml` and set an id for the `TextView`:

activity_main.xml

```
1   <TextView
2       android:id="@+id/message"
3       android:text="@string/hello_world"
4       android:layout_width="wrap_content"
5       android:layout_height="wrap_content"/>
```

At `onCreate`, try to write the id you previously chose (`message` in this example) for the `TextView`:

MainActivity.kt

```
1   override fun onCreate(savedInstanceState: Bundle?) {
2       super.onCreate(savedInstanceState)
3       setContentView(R.layout.activity_main)
4       message.text = "Hello Kotlin!"
5   }
```

Do you see the magic? You could access the view without finding it or using third-party libraries. *Kotlin Android Extensions* is a plugin that comes included in the main Kotlin one, and that is its primary purpose. Be patient; I shall show you how to use it properly soon.

You will also see that a synthetic import was added automatically to the activity, but we are not covering it yet:

MainActivity.kt

```
1   import kotlinx.android.synthetic.main.activity_main.*
```

Thanks to Kotlin interoperability with Java, we can use setters and getters methods from Java libraries as a property in Kotlin. We will talk about properties later too, but just notice that we can use message.text instead of message.setText for free. The compiler uses the real Java methods, so there is no performance overhead when using it.

Now run the app and check that everything is working fine. Review that the message TextView is showing the new content. If you have any doubts or want to revise some code, take a look at Kotlin for Android Developers repository[21]. I created a branch for each chapter when the new content involves modifications in code, so be sure to review it to check all the changes.

Next chapters cover some of the new things you could see in the converted MainActivity. Once you understand the slight differences between Java and Kotlin, you will be able to write new code by yourself without any hassle.

---

[21]https://github.com/antoniolg/Kotlin-for-Android-Developers/tree/chapter-3

4 Classes and functions

Classes in Kotlin follow a straightforward structure. However, there are some slight differences from Java that you want to know before we continue. You can use try.kotlinlang.org[22] to test this and some other simple examples without the need for a real project.

You could also use the REPL that comes bundled with the Kotlin plugin. You can find it in *Tools -> Kotlin -> Kotlin REPL*.

4.1 How to declare a class

If you want to declare a class, you just need to use the keyword `class`:

```
1   class MainActivity {
2
3   }
```

Classes have a unique default constructor. We will see that we can create extra constructors for some exceptional cases, but keep in mind that most situations only require a single constructor. Parameters are written just after the name. Braces are not required if the class is empty:

```
1   class Person(name: String, surname: String)
```

Where is the body of the constructor then? You can declare an `init` block:

---

[22]http://try.kotlinlang.org/

```
1   class Person(name: String, surname: String) {
2       init {
3       ...
4       }
5   }
```

4.2 Class inheritance

By default, a class always extends from Any (similar to Java Object), but we can extend any other classes. Classes are closed by default (final), so we can only extend a class if it is explicitly declared as open or abstract:

```
1   open class Animal(name: String)
2   class Person(firstName: String, lastName: String) : Animal(firstName)
```

Note that when using the single constructor structure, we need to specify the parameters we are using for the parent constructor. That is equivalent to calling super() in Java.

4.3 Functions

Functions (our methods in Java) are declared by using the **fun** keyword:

```
1   fun onCreate(savedInstanceState: Bundle?) {
2   }
```

Functions in Kotlin always return a value. If you skip the return value, the function is indeed returning Unit.

Unit is similar to void in Java, though this is, in fact, an object. You can, of course, specify any type as a return value:

```
1  fun add(x: Int, y: Int): Int {
2      return x + y
3  }
```

Tip: Semicolons are not necessary

As you can see in the example above, I am not using semicolons at the end of the sentences. While you can use them, semicolons are not necessary, and it is a good practice to avoid them (the IDE warns you if you write them). When you get used, you will find that it saves you loads of time.

However, if the result can be calculated using a single expression, you can get rid of brackets and use equal:

```
1  fun add(x: Int, y: Int) : Int = x + y
```

4.4 Constructor and functions parameters

Parameters in Kotlin are a bit different from Java. As you can see, we first write the name of the parameter and then its type.

```
1  fun add(x: Int, y: Int) : Int {
2      return x + y
3  }
```

A handy thing about parameters is that we can make them optional by specifying a **default value**. Here is an example of a function you could create in an activity, which uses a toast to show a message:

```
1  fun toast(message: String, length: Int = Toast.LENGTH_SHORT) {
2      Toast.makeText(this, message, length).show()
3  }
```

As you can see, the second parameter (length) specifies a default value, which allows you to write or omit the second value. This feature prevents the need for function overloading:

```
1   toast("Hello")
2   toast("Hello", Toast.LENGTH_LONG)
```

The previous function would be equivalent to the next code in Java:

```
1   void toast(String message){
2       toast(message, Toast.LENGTH_SHORT);
3   }
4
5   void toast(String message, int length){
6       Toast.makeText(this, message, length).show();
7   }
```

And this can be as complex as you want. Check this other example:

```
1   fun niceToast(message: String,
2               tag: String = MainActivity::class.java.simpleName,
3               length: Int = Toast.LENGTH_SHORT) {
4       Toast.makeText(this, "[$tag] $message", length).show()
5   }
```

I added a third parameter that includes a tag which defaults to the class name. The number of overloads we would need in Java grows exponentially. You can now write these calls:

```
1   niceToast("Hello")
2   niceToast("Hello", "MyTag")
3   niceToast("Hello", "MyTag", Toast.LENGTH_SHORT)
```

There is even another option, because you can use **named arguments**, which means you can write the name of the argument preceding the value to specify which one you want:

```
1   niceToast(message = "Hello", length = Toast.LENGTH_SHORT)
```

Tip: String templates

You can use template expressions directly in your strings, which simplifies writing complex strings based on static and variable parts. In the previous example, I used `"[$className] $message"`.

As you can see, anytime you want to add an expression, just write the `$` symbol. If the expression is a bit more complex, you can add a couple of brackets: `"Your name is ${user.name}"`.

5 Writing your first class

We already have our `MainActivity.kt` class. This activity will render a list of daily forecasts for the next seven days, so the layout requires some changes.

5.1 Creating the layout

The main view that will render the forecast list will be a `RecyclerView`, so a new dependency is required. Modify the `build.gradle` file:

app/build.gradle

```
1  dependencies {
2      compile fileTree(dir: 'libs', include: ['*.jar'])
3      compile "com.android.support:appcompat-v7:$support_version"
4      compile "com.android.support:recyclerview-v7:$support_version"
5      ...
6  }
```

Now, in `activity_main.xml` :

activity_main.xml

```
1  <FrameLayout xmlns:android="http://schemas.android.com/apk/res/android"
2               android:layout_width="match_parent"
3               android:layout_height="match_parent">
4
5      <android.support.v7.widget.RecyclerView
6          android:id="@+id/forecast_list"
7          android:layout_width="match_parent"
8          android:layout_height="match_parent"/>
9
10 </FrameLayout>
```

In `MainActivity.kt`, remove the line we added to test that everything worked (it will be showing an error now). We will continue using the good old `findViewById()` for the time being:

MainActivity.kt

```
1  val forecastList = findViewById(R.id.forecast_list) as RecyclerView
2  forecastList.layoutManager = LinearLayoutManager(this)
```

As you can see, we define the variable and cast it to `RecyclerView`. It is a bit different from Java; we are reviewing these differences in the next chapter. A `LayoutManager` is also specified, using the property naming instead of the setter. A list is enough for this layout, so let's make use of a `LinearLayoutManager`.

Object instantiation

Object instantiation presents some differences from Java too. You might have realized I omitted the "new" keyword. The constructor call is still there, but we save four precious characters. `LinearLayoutManager(this)` creates an instance of the object.

5.2 The Recycler Adapter

We need an adapter for the recycler too. I talked about `RecyclerView` on my blog[23] some time ago, so it may help you if you are not used to it.

The views used for `RecyclerView` adapter will be just `TextViews` for now, and a simple list of texts that we will create manually. Add a new Kotlin file called `ForecastListAdapter.kt`, and include this code:

---

[23]http://antonioleiva.com/recyclerview/

ForecastListAdapter.kt

```
1   class ForecastListAdapter(val items: List<String>) :
2           RecyclerView.Adapter<ForecastListAdapter.ViewHolder>() {
3
4       override fun onCreateViewHolder(parent: ViewGroup, viewType: Int):
5               ViewHolder {
6           return ViewHolder(TextView(parent.context))
7       }
8
9       override fun onBindViewHolder(holder: ViewHolder, position: Int) {
10          holder.textView.text = items[position]
11      }
12
13      override fun getItemCount(): Int = items.size
14
15      class ViewHolder(val textView: TextView) : RecyclerView.ViewHolder(textView)
16  }
```

Again, we can access the context and the text as properties. You can keep doing it as usual (using getters and setters), but you will get a warning from the compiler. This check can be disabled if you prefer to keep using the Java way. However, once you get used to properties, you will never look back.

Default visibility is public

Unless a visibility modifier is applied, classes, functions or properties are public by default. You can write it, but the compiler will show a warning, as it is not required.

If you check the previous code, you may find there are warnings for a couple of things. The first one is recommending to set the items argument to private, as it is being used only inside the class.

```
1   class ForecastListAdapter(private val items: List<String>)
```

The other is recommending to write single-lined functions using an expression body. Let's follow the recommendations here too:

```
1  override fun onCreateViewHolder(parent: ViewGroup, viewType: Int) =
2          ViewHolder(TextView(parent.context))
```

So the complete resulting code is:

ForecastListAdapter.kt

```
1  class ForecastListAdapter(private val items: List<String>)
2      : RecyclerView.Adapter<ForecastListAdapter.ViewHolder>() {
3
4      override fun onCreateViewHolder(parent: ViewGroup, viewType: Int) =
5              ViewHolder(TextView(parent.context))
6
7      override fun onBindViewHolder(holder: ViewHolder, position: Int) {
8          holder.textView.text = items[position]
9      }
10
11     override fun getItemCount(): Int = items.size
12
13     class ViewHolder(val textView: TextView) : RecyclerView.ViewHolder(textView)
14 }
```

Back to the `MainActivity`, let's create the list of strings and then an instance of the adapter:

MainActivity.kt

```
1  private val items = listOf(
2      "Mon 6/23 - Sunny - 31/17",
3      "Tue 6/24 - Foggy - 21/8",
4      "Wed 6/25 - Cloudy - 22/17",
5      "Thurs 6/26 - Rainy - 18/11",
6      "Fri 6/27 - Foggy - 21/10",
7      "Sat 6/28 - TRAPPED IN WEATHERSTATION - 23/18",
8      "Sun 6/29 - Sunny - 20/7"
9  )
10
11 override fun onCreate(savedInstanceState: Bundle?) {
12     ...
13     val forecastList = findViewById<RecyclerView>(R.id.forecast_list)
14     forecastList.layoutManager = LinearLayoutManager(this)
15     forecastList.adapter = ForecastListAdapter(items)
16 }
```

List creation

Though I will talk about collections later in this book, I just want to explain for now that you can create constant lists (called immutable, we will see this concept soon) by using the helper function `listOf`. It receives a `vararg` of items of any type and infers the type of the result.

There are many other alternative functions, such as `setOf`, `mutableListOf` or `hashSetOf`, among others.

I have also moved some classes to new packages to achieve a better project structure, so check the corresponding branch[24] if you want to follow the same organization.

We examined numerous new ideas in such a small amount of code, so let's cover them in the next chapter. We must stop here to learn some crucial concepts regarding basic types, variables, and properties.

---

[24]https://github.com/antoniolg/Kotlin-for-Android-Developers/tree/chapter-5

6 Variables and properties

In Kotlin, **everything is an object**. There are no primitive types as the ones we can use in Java. That is helpful because we have a uniform way to deal with all the available types.

6.1 Basic types

Of course, basic types such as integers, floats, characters or booleans still exist, but they all act like an object. The name of the basic types and the way they work are very similar to Java, but there are some differences you might take into account:

- There are no automatic conversions among numeric types. For instance, you cannot assign an Int to a Double variable. An explicit conversion must be done, using one of the many functions available:

```
1   val i: Int = 7
2   val d: Double = i.toDouble()
```

- Characters (Char) cannot directly be used as numbers. We can, however, convert them to a number when we need it:

```
1   val c: Char = 'c'
2   val i: Int = c.toInt()
```

- Bitwise arithmetical operations are a bit different. In Android, we use bitwise or quite often for flags, so I will stick to "and" and "or " as an example:

```
1   // Java
2   int bitwiseOr = FLAG1 | FLAG2;
3   int bitwiseAnd = FLAG1 & FLAG2;
```

```
1   // Kotlin
2   val bitwiseOr = FLAG1 or FLAG2
3   val bitwiseAnd = FLAG1 and FLAG2
```

 There are many other bitwise operations, such as `shl`, `shs`, `ushr`, `xor` or `inv`. You can take a look at the official Kotlin reference[25] for more information.

- Literals can give information about its type. It is not a requirement, but a common practice in Kotlin is to omit variable types (we will see it soon), so we can give some clues to the compiler to let it infer the type from the literal:

```
1   val i = 12 // An Int
2   val iHex = 0x0f // An Int from hexadecimal literal
3   val l = 3L // A Long
4   val d = 3.5 // A Double
5   val f = 3.5F // A Float
```

- A `String` can be accessed as an array and can be iterated:

```
1   val s = "Example"
2   val c = s[2] // This is the Char 'a'
```

---

[25]http://kotlinlang.org/docs/reference/basic-types.html#operations

```
1    // Iterate over String
2    val s = "Example"
3    for (c in s) {
4        print(c)
5    }
```

6.2 Variables

Variables in Kotlin can be easily defined as mutable (var) or immutable (val). The idea is very similar to using final in Java variables. However,**immutability** is a fundamental concept in Kotlin (and many other modern languages).

An immutable object is an object whose state cannot change after instantiation. If you need a modified version, you need to create a new object. Immutability makes software more robust and predictable. In Java, most objects are mutable, which means that any part of the code which has access to it can modify it, affecting the rest of the application.

Immutable objects are also thread-safe by definition. As the value is constant, you do not need to implement any particular synchronized mechanism, because all threads always get the same object.

So the way we think about coding changes a bit in Kotlin if we want to make use of immutability. **The key concept: just use val as much as possible.** There are situations (especially in Android, where the constructor is called by the system for several classes) where immutability becomes hard to implement, but most of the time it will be possible.

Another thing mentioned before is that we can usually avoid specifying object types, the compiler infers them from the value, which makes the code cleaner and faster to modify. We already have some examples from the section above.

```
1    val s = "Example" // A String
2    val i = 23 // An Int
3    val actionBar = supportActionBar // An ActionBar in an Activity context
```

However, a type needs to be specified if we want to use a more generic type:

```
1    val a: Any = 23
2    val c: Context = activity
```

6.3 Properties

Properties are the equivalent of fields in Java, but much more powerful. Properties do the work of a field plus a getter plus a setter. Let's see an example to compare the difference. The following snippet shows the code required in Java to access and modify a field safely:

```
1    public class Person {
2
3        private String name;
4
5        public String getName() {
6            return name;
7        }
8
9        public void setName(String name) {
10           this.name = name;
11       }
12   }
13
14   ...
15
16   Person person = new Person();
17   person.setName("name");
18   String name = person.getName();
```

In Kotlin, you only need a property to achieve the same behavior:

```
1   class Person {
2
3       var name: String = ""
4
5   }
6
7   ...
8
9   val person = Person()
10  person.name = "name"
11  val name = person.name
```

If nothing is specified, the property uses the default getter and setter. It can, of course, be modified to run whatever custom behavior you need, without having to change the existing code:

```
1   class Person {
2
3       var name: String = ""
4           get() = field.toUpperCase()
5           set(value) {
6               field = "Name: $value"
7           }
8
9   }
```

If the property needs access to its value in a custom getter or setter (as in this case), it requires the creation of a **backing field**. It can be accessed by using `field`, a reserved word, and it is automatically created when the compiler finds that it is required. Take into account that if we used the property directly, we would be using the setter and getter, and not doing a direct assignment. You can only use the backing field inside the accessors of the property.

As mentioned in some previous chapters, when dealing with code written in Java, Kotlin allows using the property syntax where a getter, and optionally a setter, are defined in Java. The compiler just links to the original getters and setters, so there are no performance penalties when using these mapped properties.

7 Anko and Extension Functions

The Kotlin team has developed some great tools to make Android development more accessible. In this chapter, I talk you about them and how you can start using them.

7.1 What is Anko?

Anko[26] is a robust library developed by JetBrains. Its primary purpose is the generation of UI layouts by using code instead of XML. This feature is interesting; try it out if you have the chance, but I will not be using it in this project. To me (probably due to years of experience writing user interfaces) using XML is more comfortable, but you might think differently.

However, this is not the only feature we can get from this library. Anko includes many helpful functions and properties that avoid lots of boilerplate. There are several examples covered in this book, but you will quickly see which kind of problems this library solves.

Since Anko is a library written specifically for Android, understanding what it does behind the scenes is a good exercise. You can navigate at any moment to Anko's source code using `ctrl + click` (Windows or Linux) or `cmd + click` (Mac). Anko's implementation is an excellent example to learn useful ways to get the most out of Kotlin language.

7.2 Start using Anko

Before going any further, let's use Anko to improve a couple of things. As you will see, anytime you use something from Anko, it includes an import with the name of the property or function to the file. Anko uses **extension functions** to add new

---
[26]https://github.com/JetBrains/anko

features to the Android framework, and the import links to them. We will see right below what an extension function is and how to write it.

In `MainActivity::onCreate`, an Anko extension function can be used instead of `findViewById` to find the `RecyclerView`. Since API 26, it is not necessary anymore, as `findViewById` is now generic, but it will serve us as an example:

activities/MainActivity.kt

```
1   val forecastList: RecyclerView = find(R.id.forecast_list)
```

Take a look at the imports, and see that the function `find` was added there:

```
1   import org.jetbrains.anko.find
```

This is all we can use from the library for now, but Anko can help us simplify, among others, the instantiation of intents, the navigation between activities, the creation of fragments, database access, or building alerts. We will find several showcase examples while we implement the app.

7.3 Extension functions

An extension function is a function that adds a new behavior to a class, even if we do not have access to the source code of that class. It is a way to extend classes which lack some useful functions. In Java, we usually implement them in utility classes which include a set of static methods. The advantage of using extension functions in Kotlin is that we don't need to pass the object as an argument. The extension function acts as part of the class, and we can implement it using `this` and all its public methods.

For instance, we can create a `toast` function that could be used by any `Context` objects and those whose type extends `Context`, such as `Activity` or `Service`:

```
1   fun Context.toast(message: CharSequence, duration: Int = Toast.LENGTH_SHORT) {
2       Toast.makeText(this, message, duration).show()
3   }
```

Now you can use this extension inside an activity, for instance:

```
1   toast("Hello world!")
2   toast("Hello world!", Toast.LENGTH_LONG)
```

Of course, Anko already includes its own toast extension function, very similar to this one. The library provides functions for both CharSequence and resources, and different names for short and long toasts:

```
1   toast("Hello world!")
2   longToast(R.string.hello_world)
```

Extensions can also be properties. So you can create extension properties in a very similar way. Thanks to this code below, you could add an extra property to ViewGroup to get a list of its child views:

```
1   val ViewGroup.childViews: List<View>
2       get() = (0 until childCount).map { getChildAt(it) }
```

Do not pay much attention to the implementation yet, as we still need to cover some of the concepts here.

Extension functions do not modify the original class. You may find a static import added to the file where you used it. You can declare extension functions anywhere, so a common practice is to create files that hold a set of related functions.

Extension functions are the magic behind many Anko features. From now on, you can create your magic too.

This chapter has little changes; you can find the source code here[27].

---

[27]https://github.com/antoniolg/Kotlin-for-Android-Developers/tree/chapter-7

8 Retrieving data from API

8.1 Performing a request

Our current placeholder texts are an excellent place to start getting an idea of what we want to achieve, but now it is time to request some real data, which will be used to populate the RecyclerView. We are going to make use of the OpenWeatherMap[28] API to retrieve data and some regular classes for the request. As Kotlin interoperability is extremely powerful, you could use any library you want, such as Retrofit[29], for server requests. However, as we are just performing a simple API request, we can achieve our goal much easier without adding another third-party library.

Besides, as you will see, Kotlin provides some extension functions that will make requests much simpler. First, we are going to create a new Request class:

data/Request.kt

```
class Request(private val url: String) {

    fun run() {
        val forecastJsonStr = URL(url).readText()
        Log.d(javaClass.simpleName, forecastJsonStr)
    }

}
```

The constructor receives a URL. Then the run function reads the result and outputs the JSON in the Logcat.

The implementation is straightforward when using readText, an extension function from the Kotlin standard library. This method is not recommended for large responses, but it is good enough in our case.

---

[28]http://openweathermap.org/
[29]https://github.com/square/retrofit

If you compare this code to the one you would need in Java, you will see that we have saved a considerable amount of overhead just by using the standard library. An `HttpURLConnection`, a `BufferedReader` and an iteration over the result would have been necessary to get the same result, apart from having to manage the status of the connection and the reader. Obviously, that is what the function is doing behind the scenes, but we have it for free.

In order to be able to perform the request, the app must use the Internet permission. So it must be added to the `AndroidManifest.xml`:

AndroidManifest.xml

```
1   <uses-permission android:name="android.permission.INTERNET" />
```

8.2 Performing the request out of the main thread

As you may know, HTTP requests are not allowed in the main thread, or the app will throw an exception. This limitation prevents from blocking the UI thread, which is a bad practice. The standard solution for Android is to use an `AsyncTask`. However, these classes are ugly and difficult to implement without any side effects. `AsyncTasks` are dangerous if not used carefully because by the time it reaches `postExecute`, the system could have destroyed the activity, and the task will crash.

Anko provides a very easy DSL to deal with asynchrony, which fits most basic needs. It provides a `doAsync` function that executes its code in another thread, with the option to return to the main thread by calling `uiThread`. Executing the request in a secondary thread is as easy as this:

activities/MainActivity.kt

```
1  val url = "http://api.openweathermap.org/data/2.5/forecast/daily?" +
2              "APPID=15646a06818f61f7b8d7823ca833e1ce&zip=94043&mode=json&units=metric&\
3  cnt=7"
4
5  doAsync() {
6      Request(url).run()
7      uiThread { longToast("Request performed") }
8  }
```

You can get the url from the repository branch[30] for this lesson.

A beautiful thing about uiThread is that it has a different implementation depending on the caller object. When an Activity uses it, the uiThread code is not executed if activity.isFinishing() returns true, and it will not crash if the activity is no longer valid.

You also can use your own executor:

```
1  val executor = Executors.newScheduledThreadPool(4)
2  doAsync(executor) {
3      // Some task
4  }
```

doAsync returns a java Future, in case you want to work with futures. If you need it to return a Future with a result, you can use doAsyncResult.

It is simple and more straightforward to read than AsyncTasks. For now, I am just sending a static URL to the request, to test that we receive the content properly and that we can draw it in the activity. I will cover the JSON parsing and conversion to app data classes soon, but before we continue, it is essential to learn what a data class is.

You can run the app and check that you can see the JSON in the log and the toast when the request finishes.

---

[30]https://github.com/antoniolg/Kotlin-for-Android-Developers/tree/chapter-8

9 Data Classes

Data classes are a powerful kind of classes that avoid the boilerplate we need in Java to create POJO: classes which are used to keep state but are elementary in the operations they do. They usually only provide plain getters and setters to access to their fields. Defining a new data class is very easy:

```
1    data class Forecast(val date: Date, val temperature: Float, val details: String)
```

9.1 Extra functions

Along with a data class, we get a handful of new functions for free, apart from the properties we already talked about (which prevent us from writing the accessors):

- equals(): it compares the properties from both objects to ensure they are identical.
- hashCode(): we get a hash code for free, also calculated from the values of the properties.
- copy(): you can copy an object, modifying the properties you need. We will see an example later.
- A set of numbered functions that are used to map an object into variables. I will also explain this soon.

9.2 Copying a data class

If we use immutability, as talked some chapters ago, we find that if we want to change the state of an object, a new instance of the class is required, with one or more of its properties modified. This task can be slightly repetitive and far from clean. However, data classes include the copy() method, which makes the process easy and intuitive.

For instance, if we need to modify the temperature of a Forecast, we can just do:

```
1    val f1 = Forecast(Date(), 27.5f, "Shiny day")
2    val f2 = f1.copy(temperature = 30f)
```

This way, we copy the first forecast and modify only the temperature property without changing the state of the original object.

 ## Be careful with immutability when using Java classes

If you decide to work with immutability, be aware that Java classes were not designed with this in mind, and there are still some circumstances where you are able to modify the state. In the previous example, you could always access the Date object and change its value. The easy (and unsafe) option is to remember the rules of not modifying the state of an object, but copying it when necessary.

Another option is to wrap these classes. You could create an ImmutableDate class which wraps a Date and does not allow to modify its state. It is up to you to decide which solution you take. In this book, I am not very strict with immutability. So I will not create wrappers for every potentially dangerous class.

9.3 Mapping an object into variables

This process is known as **declaration destructuring**, and consists of mapping each property inside an object into a variable. That is the reason why the componentX functions are automatically created. An example with the previous Forecast class:

```
1    val f1 = Forecast(Date(), 27.5f, "Shiny day")
2    val (date, temperature, details) = f1
```

This multi-declaration is compiled down to the following code:

```
1   val date = f1.component1()
2   val temperature = f1.component2()
3   val details = f1.component3()
```

The logic behind this feature is powerful and can help simplify the code in many situations. For instance, `Map` class has some extension functions implemented that allow recovering its keys and values in an iteration:

```
1   for ((key, value) in map) {
2       Log.d("map", "key:$key, value:$value")
3   }
```

10 Parsing data

Now that we know how to create data classes, we are ready to start parsing data. In the data package, create a new file called ResponseClasses.kt. If you open in a browser the URL we used in chapter 8, you can see the structure of the JSON file. It consists of an object which contains a city, and a list of forecast predictions. The city has an id, a name, its coordinates and the country where it belongs. Each forecast comes with a good set of information such as the date, different temperatures, and a weather object with the description and an id for an icon, for instance.

10.1 Converting JSON to data classes

In our current UI, we are not going to use all this data. However, we will parse everything down to classes, in case it is of some use in the future. These are the data classes we need:

data/ResponseClasses.kt

```
1   data class ForecastResult(val city: City, val list: List<Forecast>)
2
3   data class City(val id: Long, val name: String, val coord: Coordinates,
4                   val country: String, val population: Int)
5
6   data class Coordinates(val lon: Float, val lat: Float)
7
8   data class Forecast(val dt: Long, val temp: Temperature, val pressure: Float,
9                       val humidity: Int, val weather: List<Weather>,
10                      val speed: Float, val deg: Int, val clouds: Int,
11                      val rain: Float)
12
13  data class Temperature(val day: Float, val min: Float, val max: Float,
14                         val night: Float, val eve: Float, val morn: Float)
15
16  data class Weather(val id: Long, val main: String, val description: String,
17                     val icon: String)
```

As we are using Gson[31] to parse the JSON to our classes, the properties must have the same name as the ones in the JSON or specify a serialized name. A good practice explained in most software architectures is to use different models for the different layers in our app to decouple them from each other. So I prefer to simplify the declaration of these classes because I will convert them before being used in the rest of the app. The names of the properties used in this class are the same as the names in the JSON response.

Now, the Request class needs some modifications to return the parsed result. It also receives only the zipcode of the city instead of the complete URL so that it becomes more readable. For now, the static URL is declared in a **companion object**.

Companion objects

Kotlin allows declaring objects to define static behaviors. In Kotlin, we cannot create static properties or functions, but we need to rely on objects. However, these objects make some well-known patterns such as Singleton very easy to implement.

If we need some static properties, constants or functions in a class, we can use a **companion object**. This object is shared among all instances of the class, the same as a static field or method would do in Java. Use the reserved word const for your compile-time constants. They are more efficient and friendly to use from Java code.

Check the resulting code:

data/ForecastRequest.kt

```
1   class ForecastRequest(private val zipCode: String) {
2
3       companion object {
4           private const val APP_ID = "15646a06818f61f7b8d7823ca833e1ce"
5           private const val URL = "http://api.openweathermap.org/data/2.5/" +
6                   "forecast/daily?mode=json&units=metric&cnt=7"
7           private const val COMPLETE_URL = "$URL&APPID=$APP_ID&zip="
8       }
9
10      fun execute(): ForecastResult {
```

[31]https://github.com/google/gson

```
11        val forecastJsonStr = URL(COMPLETE_URL + zipCode).readText()
12        return Gson().fromJson(forecastJsonStr, ForecastResult::class.java)
13    }
14 }
```

Remember you need to add the Gson library to `build.gradle` dependencies:

app/build.gradle

```
1 compile "com.google.code.gson:gson:2.8.5"
```

10.2 Shaping the domain layer

Now let's create a new package representing the `domain` layer. It contains some Commands in charge of performing the use cases of the app.

Firstly, a definition of a Command is required. There is a generic declaration in the following example. We will talk about this topic in next chapters.

domain/commands/Command.kt

```
1 public interface Command<out T> {
2     fun execute(): T
3 }
```

These commands execute an operation and return an object of the class specified in its generic type. Remember that **every function in Kotlin returns a value**. By default, if nothing is specified, it returns an object of the Unit class. So if we want our Command to return nothing, we can specify Unit as its type.

Interfaces in Kotlin are more potent than Java (before Java 8) because they can contain code. However, for now, we do not need that feature.

The first command needs to request the forecast to the API and convert it to domain classes. This is the definition of the domain classes:

domain/model/DomainClasses.kt

```
1   data class ForecastList(val city: String, val country: String,
2                           val dailyForecast:List<Forecast>)
3
4   data class Forecast(val date: String, val description: String, val high: Int,
5                       val low: Int)
```

These classes will probably need to be reviewed in the future when we add more features. For now, the data they keep is enough.

Classes must be mapped from the data to the domain model, so the next task will be to create a DataMapper:

domain/mappers/ForecastDataMapper.kt

```
1   class ForecastDataMapper {
2
3       fun convertFromDataModel(forecast: ForecastResult): ForecastList =
4           ForecastList(forecast.city.name, forecast.city.country,
5               convertForecastListToDomain(forecast.list))
6
7       private fun convertForecastListToDomain(list: List<Forecast>)
8               : List<ModelForecast> {
9           return list.mapIndexed { i, forecast ->
10              val dt = Calendar.getInstance().timeInMillis +
11                  TimeUnit.DAYS.toMillis(i.toLong())
12              convertForecastItemToDomain(forecast.copy(dt = dt))
13          }
14      }
15
16      private fun convertForecastItemToDomain(forecast: Forecast): ModelForecast {
17          return ModelForecast(convertDate(forecast.dt),
18                  forecast.weather[0].description, forecast.temp.max.toInt(),
19                  forecast.temp.min.toInt())
20      }
21
22      private fun convertDate(date: Long): String {
23          val df = DateFormat.getDateInstance(DateFormat.MEDIUM, Locale.getDefault())
24          return df.format(date)
25      }
26  }
```

As we are using two classes with the same name, give a specific name to one of them so that we can avoid writing the complete package:

```
1   import com.antonioleiva.weatherapp.domain.model.Forecast as ModelForecast
```

Another interesting point about this code is the way to convert the forecast list from the data to the domain model:

```
1   return list.mapIndexed { i, forecast -> ... }
```

We can loop over the collection that easily and return a new list with the converted items. Kotlin provides a good set of functional operations over lists, which apply an operation for all the items in a list and transform them in any way. Collection operations are one of the most powerful features in Kotlin for developers used to Java 7. We shall take a look at all the different transformations very soon. It is important to know they exist because it makes it easier to find places where these functions can save much time and boilerplate.

You may have noticed too that I am not using the date, but generating a new one. That is because the request returns a date that is difficult to convert correctly to current date while not having issues with timezone. As we know that the first day we receive is today, we can iterate and build the proper dates this way.

And now, everything is ready to write the command:

domain/commands/RequestForecastCommand.kt

```
1   class RequestForecastCommand(private val zipCode: String) :
2           Command<ForecastList> {
3       override fun execute(): ForecastList {
4           val forecastRequest = ForecastRequest(zipCode)
5           return ForecastDataMapper().convertFromDataModel(
6                   forecastRequest.execute())
7       }
8   }
```

10.3 Drawing the data in the UI

`MainActivity` code changes a little, because now we have real data to fill the adapter. The asynchronous call needs to be rewritten:

ui/activities/MainActivity.kt

```
1   doAsync() {
2       val result = RequestForecastCommand("94043").execute()
3       uiThread {
4           forecastList.adapter = ForecastListAdapter(result)
5       }
6   }
```

The adapter requires some modifications too:

ui/adapters/ForecastListAdapter.kt

```
1   class ForecastListAdapter(private  val weekForecast: ForecastList) :
2           RecyclerView.Adapter<ForecastListAdapter.ViewHolder>() {
3
4       override fun onCreateViewHolder(parent: ViewGroup, viewType: Int):
5               ViewHolder? {
6           return ViewHolder(TextView(parent.getContext()))
7       }
8
9       override fun onBindViewHolder(holder: ViewHolder,
10              position: Int) {
11          with(weekForecast.dailyForecast[position]) {
12              holder.textView.text = "$date - $description - $high/$low"
13          }
14      }
15
16      override fun getItemCount(): Int = weekForecast.dailyForecast.size
17
18      class ViewHolder(val textView: TextView) : RecyclerView.ViewHolder(textView)
19  }
```

with **function**

with is a useful function included in the standard Kotlin library. It receives an object and an extension function as parameters and makes the object execute the function. That way, all the code that we define inside the brackets acts as an extension function for the object provided in the first parameter, and we can use all its public functions and properties, as well as this. The with function is helpful to simplify code when we do several operations over the same object.

There is some new code in this chapter, so feel free to check it out on the repository[32].

---

[32]https://github.com/antoniolg/Kotlin-for-Android-Developers/tree/chapter-10

11 Operator overloading

Kotlin has a fixed number of symbolic operators we can use in any class. These symbols map to a function, which is the one that provides the logic that the operator uses. Overloading these operators may increment the readability and simplicity of your code.

To notify the compiler that you want to overload an operator, you must annotate the functions with the `operator` modifier.

11.1 Operators tables

Here you can see a set of tables that include an operator and its corresponding function. A function with that name must be implemented to enable the possibility of using the operator in a specific class.

Unary operations

+a	a.unaryPlus()
-a	a.unaryMinus()
!a	a.not()
a++	a.inc()
a−	a.dec()

Binary operations

a + b	a.plus(b)
a - b	a.minus(b)
a * b	a.times(b)
a / b	a.div(b)
a % b	a.mod(b)
a..b	a.rangeTo(b)
a in b	b.contains(a)
a !in b	!b.contains(a)
a += b	a.plusAssign(b)
a -= b	a.minusAssign(b)
a *= b	a.timesAssign(b)
a /= b	a.divAssign(b)
a %= b	a.modAssign(b)

Array-like operations

a[i]	a.get(i)
a[i, j]	a.get(i, j)
a[i_1, ..., i_n]	a.get(i_1, ..., i_n)
a[i] = b	a.set(i, b)
a[i, j] = b	a.set(i, j, b)
a[i_1, ..., i_n] = b	a.set(i_1, ..., i_n, b)

Equals operation

a == b	a?.equals(b) ?: b === null
a != b	!(a?.equals(b) ?: b === null)

The equals operations are a bit different, because they use a more complex translation to make a proper equals checking, and because they expect an exact function specification and not just a specific name. The function must be implemented exactly like this:

```
operator fun equals(other: Any?): Boolean
```

Operators === and !== do identity checks (they are == and != in Java respectively) and cannot be overloaded.

Function invocation

a(i)   a.invoke(i)
a(i, j)   a.invoke(i, j)
a(i_1, ..., i_n)   a.invoke(i_1, ..., i_n)

11.2 An example

As you can imagine, Kotlin lists have the array-like operations implemented in the standard library, so we can access the items of the list the same way we would do in Java arrays. But it goes beyond: in mutable lists, you can also assign a value to a position by using the same operator:

```
1  val x = myList[2]
2  myList[2] = 4
```

If you remember, we have a data class called ForecastList, which consists of a list with some extra info. It would be interesting to access its items directly instead of having to request its internal list to get an item. On an unrelated note, I am also going to implement a size property, which simplifies the current adapter a little more:

domain/model/DomainClasses.kt

```
1  data class ForecastList(val city: String, val country: String,
2      private val dailyForecast: List<Forecast>) {
3
4      val size: Int
5          get() = dailyForecast.size
6
7      operator fun get(position: Int): Forecast = dailyForecast[position]
8  }
```

It makes our onBindViewHolder a bit simpler:

ui/adapters/ForecastListAdapter.kt

```
1  override fun onBindViewHolder(holder: ViewHolder, position: Int) {
2      with(weekForecast[position]) {
3          holder.textView.text = "$date - $description - $high/$low"
4      }
5  }
```

As well as the getItemCount() function:

ui/adapters/ForecastListAdapter.kt

```
1  override fun getItemCount(): Int = weekForecast.size
```

11.3 Operators in extension functions

Apart from using extension functions for our classes, we can also extend existing classes to provide new operations to third-party libraries. For instance, we could access to ViewGroup views the same way we do with lists:

```
1  operator fun ViewGroup.get(position: Int): View
2          = getChildAt(position)
```

Now it is really simple to get a view from a ViewGroup by its position:

```
1  val container: ViewGroup = find(R.id.container)
2  val view = container[2]
```

Take a look at the branch for this chapter[33], and then you can go on with the next one.

---

[33]https://github.com/antoniolg/Kotlin-for-Android-Developers/tree/chapter-11

12 Making the forecast list clickable

Current items layout needs some work to be ready for a real app. The first thing is to create a proper XML that can fit our basic needs. We want to show an icon, date, description and high and low temperatures. So let's create a layout called item_-forecast.xml:

layout/item_forecast.xml

```
1   <?xml version="1.0" encoding="utf-8"?>
2   <LinearLayout
3       xmlns:android="http://schemas.android.com/apk/res/android"
4       xmlns:tools="http://schemas.android.com/tools"
5       android:layout_width="match_parent"
6       android:layout_height="match_parent"
7       android:padding="@dimen/spacing_xlarge"
8       android:background="?attr/selectableItemBackground"
9       android:gravity="center_vertical"
10      android:orientation="horizontal">
11
12      <ImageView
13          android:id="@+id/icon"
14          android:layout_width="48dp"
15          android:layout_height="48dp"
16          tools:src="@mipmap/ic_launcher"/>
17
18      <LinearLayout
19          android:layout_width="0dp"
20          android:layout_height="wrap_content"
21          android:layout_weight="1"
22          android:layout_marginLeft="@dimen/spacing_xlarge"
23          android:layout_marginRight="@dimen/spacing_xlarge"
24          android:orientation="vertical">
25
26          <TextView
27              android:id="@+id/date"
28              android:layout_width="match_parent"
```

```
29            android:layout_height="wrap_content"
30            android:textAppearance="@style/TextAppearance.AppCompat.Medium"
31            tools:text="May 14, 2015"/>
32
33        <TextView
34            android:id="@+id/description"
35            android:layout_width="match_parent"
36            android:layout_height="wrap_content"
37            android:textAppearance="@style/TextAppearance.AppCompat.Caption"
38            tools:text="Light Rain"/>
39
40    </LinearLayout>
41
42    <LinearLayout
43        android:layout_width="wrap_content"
44        android:layout_height="wrap_content"
45        android:gravity="center_horizontal"
46        android:orientation="vertical">
47
48        <TextView
49            android:id="@+id/maxTemperature"
50            android:layout_width="wrap_content"
51            android:layout_height="wrap_content"
52            android:textAppearance="@style/TextAppearance.AppCompat.Medium"
53            tools:text="30"/>
54
55        <TextView
56            android:id="@+id/minTemperature"
57            android:layout_width="wrap_content"
58            android:layout_height="wrap_content"
59            android:textAppearance="@style/TextAppearance.AppCompat.Caption"
60            tools:text="15"/>
61
62    </LinearLayout>
63
64 </LinearLayout>
```

The domain model and data mapper must generate the complete icon url, so that we can load it:

model/DomainClasses.kt

```
1   data class Forecast(val date: String, val description: String,
2                       val high: Int, val low: Int, val iconUrl: String)
```

In ForecastDataMapper:

domain/mappers/ForecastDataMapper.kt

```
1   private fun convertForecastItemToDomain(forecast: Forecast): ModelForecast {
2       return ModelForecast(convertDate(forecast.dt),
3               forecast.weather[0].description, forecast.temp.max.toInt(),
4               forecast.temp.min.toInt(), generateIconUrl(forecast.weather[0].icon))
5   }
6
7   private fun generateIconUrl(iconCode: String): String
8           = "http://openweathermap.org/img/w/$iconCode.png"
```

The icon code we got from the first request is used to compose the complete URL for the icon image. The simplest way to load an image is by making use of an image loader library. Picasso[34] is an excellent option. You must add it to build.gradle dependencies:

app/build.gradle

```
1   compile "com.squareup.picasso:picasso:2.5.2"
```

The adapter needs a big rework too. A click listener will be necessary, so let's define it:

ui/adapters/ForecastListAdapter.kt

```
1   interface OnItemClickListener {
2       operator fun invoke(forecast: Forecast)
3   }
```

If you remember from the last lesson, you can omit the invoke method when calling it. So let's use it as a way of simplification. The listener can be called in two ways:

---

[34]http://square.github.io/picasso/

```
1    itemClick.invoke(forecast)
2    itemClick(forecast)
```

The `ViewHolder` will now be responsible of binding the forecast to the new view:

ui/adapters/ForecastListAdapter.kt

```
1    class ViewHolder(view: View, private val itemClick: OnItemClickListener)
2        : RecyclerView.ViewHolder(view) {
3
4        private val iconView = view.find<ImageView>(R.id.icon)
5        private val dateView = view.find<TextView>(R.id.date)
6        private val descriptionView =
7                view.find<TextView>(R.id.description)
8        private val maxTemperatureView =
9                view.find<TextView>(R.id.maxTemperature)
10       private val minTemperatureView =
11               view.find<TextView>(R.id.minTemperature)
12
13       fun bindForecast(forecast: Forecast) {
14           with(forecast) {
15               Picasso.with(itemView.ctx).load(iconUrl).into(iconView)
16               dateView.text = date
17               descriptionView.text = description
18               maxTemperatureView.text = "$high"
19               minTemperatureView.text = "$low"
20               itemView.setOnClickListener { itemClick(this) }
21           }
22       }
23   }
```

The constructor of the adapter now receives the `itemClick`. The methods for creation and binding are simpler:

ui/adapters/ForecastListAdapter.kt

```
1    public class ForecastListAdapter(private val weekForecast: ForecastList,
2            private val itemClick: ForecastListAdapter.OnItemClickListener) :
3            RecyclerView.Adapter<ForecastListAdapter.ViewHolder>() {
4
5        override fun onCreateViewHolder(parent: ViewGroup, viewType: Int):
6                ViewHolder {
7            val view = LayoutInflater.from(parent.ctx)
8                .inflate(R.layout.item_forecast, parent, false)
9
10           return ViewHolder(view, itemClick)
11       }
12
13       override fun onBindViewHolder(holder: ViewHolder, position: Int) {
14           holder.bindForecast(weekForecast[position])
15       }
16       ...
17   }
```

If you use this code, `parent.ctx` will not compile. Anko provides many extension functions to make Android coding simpler. It, for instance, includes a `ctx` property for activities and fragments, among others, which returns the context, but it lacks the same property for views. So we are going to create a new file called `ViewExtensions.kt` inside `ui.utils`, and add this extension property:

```
1    val View.ctx: Context
2        get() = context
```

From now on, any view can make use of it. It is not necessary at all, because you can use `context` synthetic property, but I think it gives some consistency if we are planning to use `ctx` in the other classes. Besides, it is another example of how to use extension properties.

Finally, the `MainActivity` call to `setAdapter` results into this:

ui/activities/MainActivity.kt

```
1  forecastList.adapter = ForecastListAdapter(result,
2        object : ForecastListAdapter.OnItemClickListener{
3            override fun invoke(forecast: Forecast) {
4                toast(forecast.date)
5            }
6        })
```

As you can see, to implement an anonymous class we, in fact, create an `object` that implements the interface we created. That is because we are not making use of the power of functional programming, but you will learn how to convert this code into something cleaner in the next chapter.

Try the new changes from the repository[35].

---

[35]https://github.com/antoniolg/Kotlin-for-Android-Developers/tree/chapter-12

13 Lambdas

A lambda expression is a simple way to define an anonymous function. Lambdas are very useful because they prevent us from having to write the specification of the function in an abstract class or interface, and then the implementation of the class.

In Kotlin, lambdas are first class citizens, which means that a function behaves as a type: it can be passed as an argument to another function, can be returned by a function, saved into a variable or a property, etc.

13.1 Simplifying setOnClickListener()

Let's see how this works using a typical example in Android: the click listener method from a View. If we want to implement a click listener behavior in Java, we first need to write the OnClickListener interface:

```
1   public interface OnClickListener {
2       void onClick(View v);
3   }
```

And then we write an anonymous class that implements this interface:

```
1   view.setOnClickListener(new OnClickListener() {
2       @Override
3       public void onClick(View v) {
4           Toast.makeText(v.getContext(), "Click", Toast.LENGTH_SHORT).show();
5       }
6   });
```

This would be the transformation of the code into Kotlin (using toast function from Anko):

```
1   view.setOnClickListener(object : OnClickListener {
2       override fun onClick(v: View) {
3           toast("Click")
4       }
5   })
```

Luckily, Kotlin allows some optimizations over Java libraries, and lambdas can substitute any function that receives an interface with a single function. It works as if we had defined setOnclickListener() like this:

```
1   fun setOnClickListener(listener: (View) -> Unit)
```

To define a lambda expression, specify the function input arguments to the left of the arrow (surrounded by parentheses), and the return type to the right. In this case, we get a View and return Unit (nothing). So with this in mind, we can simplify the previous code a little:

```
1   view.setOnClickListener({ view -> toast("Click")})
```

Nice difference! While defining a function, we must use braces and specify the argument values to the left of the arrow and the body of the function to the right. We can even get rid of the left part if the input values are not used:

```
1   view.setOnClickListener({ toast("Click") })
```

If the last argument of a function is also a function, we can move it out of the parentheses:

```
1   view.setOnClickListener() { toast("Click") }
```

And, finally, if the function is the only parameter, we can get rid of the parentheses:

```
1   view.setOnClickListener { toast("Click") }
```

More than five times smaller than the original code in Java, and much easier to understand what is doing.

13.2 Click listener for ForecastListAdapter

In the previous chapter, I wrote the click listener the hard way on purpose to have a good context to develop this one. But now it is time to put what you learnt into practice. We are removing the listener interface from the ForecastListAdapter and using a lambda instead:

ui/adapters/ForecastListAdapter.kt

```
public class ForecastListAdapter(private val weekForecast: ForecastList,
                                 private val itemClick: (Forecast) -> Unit)
```

The function will receive a forecast and return nothing. The same change can be done to the ViewHolder:

ui/adapters/ForecastListAdapter.kt

```
class ViewHolder(view: View, private val itemClick: (Forecast) -> Unit)
```

The rest of the code remains unmodified. Just a last change to MainActivity:

ui/activities/MainActivity.kt

```
val adapter = ForecastListAdapter(result) { forecast -> toast(forecast.date) }
```

We can simplify the last line even more. In lambdas with only one argument, we can make use of the *it* reference, which prevents us from defining the left part of the function specifically. So we can do:

```
val adapter = ForecastListAdapter(result) { toast(it.date) }
```

13.3 Extending the language

Thanks to these transformations, we can create our builders and code blocks. We have already been using some interesting functions such as with. Though the one included in the standard library is a little more complex, a simpler implementation would be:

```
1    inline fun <T> with(t: T, body: T.() -> Unit) { t.body() }
```

This function gets an object of type `T` and a lambda that behaves as an extension function. The implementation takes the object and lets it execute the function. As the second parameter of the function is another function, it can be brought out of the parentheses, so we can create a block of code where we can use `this` and the public properties and functions of the object directly:

```
1    with(forecast) {
2        Picasso.with(itemView.ctx).load(iconUrl).into(iconView)
3        dateView.text = date
4        descriptionView.text = description
5        maxTemperatureView.text = "$high"
6        minTemperatureView.text = "$low"
7        itemView.setOnClickListener { itemClick(this) }
8    }
```

Inline functions

Inline functions are a bit different from regular functions. An inline function is substituted by its code during compilation, instead of doing the real call to a function. That reduces memory allocations and runtime overhead in some situations. For instance, if we have a function as an argument, a regular function internally creates an object that contains that function. On the other hand, inline functions substitute the code of the function in the place where it is called, so it does not require an internal object for that.

Another example: we could create blocks of code that only run if the version is Lollipop or newer:

```
1   inline fun supportsLollipop(code: () -> Unit) {
2       if (Build.VERSION.SDK_INT >= Build.VERSION_CODES.LOLLIPOP) {
3           code()
4       }
5   }
```

The body of the function checks the version and executes the code if it meets the requirements. Now we could do:

```
1   supportsLollipop {
2       window.setStatusBarColor(Color.BLACK)
3   }
```

For instance, Anko is also based on this idea to implement the DSL for Android layouts. You can also check an example from Kotlin reference, a showcase of a DSL to generate HTML[36] from code.

The changes from this chapter are in its corresponding branch[37].

---

[36]http://kotlinlang.org/docs/reference/type-safe-builders.html

[37]https://github.com/antoniolg/Kotlin-for-Android-Developers/tree/chapter-13

14 Visibility Modifiers

Modifiers are a bit different in Kotlin from how we use them in Java. The default modifier in this language is public, which saves a lot of time and characters. Here it is the long explanation: how do visibility modifiers work in Kotlin?

14.1 Modifiers

private

The private modifier is the most restrictive we can use. It indicates it is visible in its file. So if we declare a class as private, we are not able to use it outside the file where it was defined.

On the other hand, if we use private inside a class, the access is restricted to that class. Even classes that extend it cannot use it.

So first level classes, objects, interfaces... (known as package members) declared as private are only visible inside the file where they are declared, while everything defined inside a class or interface is only visible by that class or interface.

protected

This modifier only applies to members of a class or an interface. A package member cannot be protected. Inside a member, it works the same way as in Java: it can be used by the member itself and the members that extend it (for instance, a class and its subclasses).

internal

An internal member is visible inside the whole module if it is a package member. If it is a member of another scope, it depends on the visibility of the scope. For instance, if we write a private class, the access to an `internal` function is limited to the visibility of the class.

We can use internal classes from any other class in the same module, but not from another module.

What is a module?

According to Jetbrains definition, a module is a discrete unit of functionality which you can compile, run, test and debug independently. It refers to the Android Studio modules we can create to split our project into different blocks. In Eclipse, these modules would refer to the projects inside a workspace.

public

As you may guess, this is the less restrictive modifier. ** It is the default modifier**, and a member declared as `public` is visible anywhere, only restricted by its scope. A public member defined in a private class will not be visible outside the scope where the class is visible.

14.2 Constructors

By default, all constructors are `public`, which means they can be used from any scope where their class is visible. If we want to restrict the visibility of a constructor, we can apply modifiers to it with this specific syntax:

```
1   class C private constructor(a: Int) { ... }
```

14.3 Reviewing our code

We already made use of the `public` default modifier, and latest versions of the Kotlin plugin also detect when an argument can be private. For instance, in `RequestForecastCommand`, we made the `zipCode` property private.

```
1   class RequestForecastCommand(private val zipCode: String)
```

Besides, in Kotlin we do not need to specify the return type of a function if the compiler can infer it. An example of how we can get rid of the returning types:

```
1   data class ForecastList(...) {
2       operator fun get(position: Int) = dailyForecast[position]
3   }
```

The typical situations where we can get rid of the return type are when we assign the value to a function or a property using equals (=) instead of writing a code block.

The rest of the modifications are pretty straightforward. You can review them in the repository[38].

---

[38]https://github.com/antoniolg/Kotlin-for-Android-Developers/tree/chapter-14

15 Kotlin Android Extensions

Kotlin Android Extensions is another plugin that the Kotlin team has developed to make Android development simpler. The plugin automatically creates a set of properties that give direct access to all the views in the XML. This way we do not need to explicitly find all the views in the layout before starting using them.

The names of the properties are taken from the ids of the views, so we must be careful when choosing those names because they now become a relevant part of our base code. The plugin also infers the type of these properties from the XML, so there is no need to do any extra castings.

Kotlin Android Extensions is that it does not require adding libraries to our project. The plugin generates the code it needs to work only when it is required.

How does it work under the hood? These properties delegate to functions that request the view, and a caching function that prevents from doing a `findViewById` every time a property is used. Be aware that this caching mechanism only works if the receiver is an Activity or a Fragment. It skips the cache if it is inside an extension function because the plugin is not able to add the necessary code.

15.1 How to use Kotlin Android Extensions

Let's see how easy it is. Though the plugin is part of the regular one (it does not require to install a new one), if you want to use it you have to add an extra *apply* in the Android module:

app/build.gradle

```
1   apply plugin: 'com.android.application'
2   apply plugin: 'kotlin-android'
3   apply plugin: 'kotlin-android-extensions'
```

If you remember, we already did that at the beginning of the book.

Recovering views from the XML

From this moment, recovering a view is as easy as **using the view id you defined in the XML directly into your activity**. Imagine you have an XML like this one:

```
1   <FrameLayout
2       xmlns:android="http://schemas.android.com/apk/res/android"
3       android:layout_width="match_parent"
4       android:layout_height="match_parent">
5
6       <TextView
7           android:id="@+id/welcomeMessage"
8           android:layout_width="wrap_content"
9           android:layout_height="wrap_content"
10          android:layout_gravity="center"
11          android:text="Hello World!"/>
12
13  </FrameLayout>
```

As you can see, the TextView has welcomeMessage id. In the MainActivity you now could write:

```
1   override fun onCreate(savedInstanceState: Bundle?) {
2       super.onCreate(savedInstanceState)
3       setContentView(R.layout.activity_main)
4
5       welcomeMessage.text = "Hello Kotlin!"
6   }
```

To use it, you require a special *import* (the one I write below), but the IDE can write the import for you:

```
1   import kotlinx.android.synthetic.main.activity_main.*
```

The new Android Studio activity templates now include nested layouts, by using the `include` tag. It is important to know that you must add a synthetic import for each XML you use:

```
1   import kotlinx.android.synthetic.main.activity_main.*
2   import kotlinx.android.synthetic.main.content_main.*
```

As I mentioned above, the generated code includes a view cache. So if you ask for the view again, this does not require another `findViewById`. Let's see what it is doing behind the scenes.

The magic behind Kotlin Android Extensions

When you start working with Kotlin, it is helpful to understand the bytecode generated when you use a new feature. This practice helps you understand the hidden costs of your decisions.

There is an action below *Tools –> Kotlin*, called *Show Kotlin Bytecode* . If you click here, you can see the bytecode generated when the class file you opened is compiled.

The bytecode is not helpful for most humans, but there is another option here: *Decompile*.

This section shows a Java representation of the bytecode generated by Kotlin. That way, you can compare the Java equivalent to the Kotlin code you wrote.

I am going to use this on the previous sample activity, and see the code generated by Kotlin Android Extensions.

The interesting part is this one:

```
1   ...
2   public View _$_findCachedViewById(int var1) {
3       if(this._$_findViewCache == null) {
4           this._$_findViewCache = new HashMap();
5       }
6
7       View var2 = (View)this._$_findViewCache.get(Integer.valueOf(var1));
8       if(var2 == null) {
9           var2 = this.findViewById(var1);
10          this._$_findViewCache.put(Integer.valueOf(var1), var2);
11      }
12
13      return var2;
14  }
15
16  public void _$_clearFindViewByIdCache() {
17      if(this._$_findViewCache != null) {
18          this._$_findViewCache.clear();
19      }
20
21  }
```

Here it is the view cache we were talking about. When a view is requested, it tries to find it in the cache. If it is not there, it uses findViewById and adds it to the cache. Pretty simple indeed.

Besides, it adds a function to clear the cache: clearFindViewByIdCache(). You can use it for instance if you rebuild the view, as the old views are not valid anymore. Then this line:

```
1   welcomeMessage.text = "Hello Kotlin!"
```

is converted into this:

```
1   ((TextView)this._$_findCachedViewById(id.welcomeMessage))
2       .setText((CharSequence)"Hello Kotlin!");
```

So the properties are not real, the plugin is not generating a property per view. It replaces the code during compilation to access the view cache, cast it to the proper type and call the method.

Kotlin Android Extensions on fragments

Fragments can also use this plugin. The problem with fragments is that the view can be recreated while the fragment instance keeps alive. What happens then? This means that the views inside the cache would no longer be valid.

Let's see the code it generates if we use a fragment. I am creating this simple fragment, that uses the same XML I wrote above:

```kotlin
class Fragment : Fragment() {

    override fun onCreateView(inflater: LayoutInflater, container: ViewGroup?,
            savedInstanceState: Bundle?): View? {
        return inflater.inflate(R.layout.fragment, container, false)
    }

    override fun onViewCreated(view: View?, savedInstanceState: Bundle?) {
        super.onViewCreated(view, savedInstanceState)
        welcomeMessage.text = "Hello Kotlin!"
    }
}
```

In onViewCreated, I change the text of the TextView. What about the generated bytecode? Everything is the same as in the activity, with this slight difference:

```java
// $FF: synthetic method
public void onDestroyView() {
    super.onDestroyView();
    this._$_clearFindViewByIdCache();
}
```

When the view is destroyed, this method calls clearFindViewByIdCache, so we are safe here.

Kotlin Android extensions on a Custom View

It will work very similarly on a custom view. Imagine we have a view like this:

```
1   <merge xmlns:android="http://schemas.android.com/apk/res/android"
2                 android:orientation="vertical"
3                 android:layout_width="match_parent"
4                 android:layout_height="match_parent">
5
6       <ImageView
7           android:id="@+id/itemImage"
8           android:layout_width="match_parent"
9           android:layout_height="200dp"/>
10
11      <TextView
12          android:id="@+id/itemTitle"
13          android:layout_width="match_parent"
14          android:layout_height="wrap_content"/>
15
16  </merge>
```

I am creating a straightforward custom view and generating the constructors with the new intent that uses @JvmOverloads annotation. When a class extends a View or a subclass of it, you can press *Alt + Enter*, where you find the option to create a constructor like this:

```
1   class CustomView @JvmOverloads constructor(
2           context: Context, attrs: AttributeSet? = null, defStyleAttr: Int = 0
3   ) : LinearLayout(context, attrs, defStyleAttr) {
4
5       init {
6           LayoutInflater.from(context).inflate(R.layout.view_custom, this, true)
7           itemTitle.text = "Hello Kotlin!"
8       }
9   }
```

At the end of the book, I will tell you more about these annotations and how to use them to improve the interoperability with Java code.

In the example above, I am modifying the text of itemTitle. The generated code should be trying to find the view from the cache. It does not make sense to copy all the same decompiled code again, but you can see this in the line that modifies the text:

```
1   ((TextView)this._$_findCachedViewById(id.itemTitle))
2       .setText((CharSequence)"Hello Kotlin!");
```

We are only calling `findViewById` first time in custom views too.

Recovering views from another view

The last alternative Kotlin Android Extensions provide is to use the properties directly from another view. I am using a layout very similar to the one in the previous section. Imagine that this is inflated in an adapter for instance. You can also access the subviews directly, just by using this plugin:

```
1   val itemView = ...
2   itemView.itemImage.setImageResource(R.drawable.image)
3   itemView.itemTitle.text = "My Text"
```

The plugin also helps you fill the *import*. Check that this one is different:

```
1   import kotlinx.android.synthetic.main.view_item.view.*
```

There are a couple of things you need to know about this:

- In compilation time, you can reference any views from any other views. This means you could be referencing a view that is not a direct child of that one. Of course, this crashes in execution time when it tries to recover a view that does not exist.
- In this case, views are not cached, as opposed to *Activities* and *Fragments*.

Why is this? Here the plugin does not have a place to generate the required code for the cache. If you again review the code that is generated by the plugin when calling a property from a view, you will see this:

```
1   ((TextView)itemView.findViewById(id.itemTitle)).setText((CharSequence)"My Text");
```

As you can see, there is no call to a cache. Be careful if your view is complex and you are using this in an adapter. It might impact the performance.

Alternatively, if you are using Kotlin 1.1.4 or newer, you have another option.

15.2 Kotlin Android Extensions in 1.1.4

From this version of Kotlin, the Android Extensions have incorporated some new exciting features: caches in any classes, and a new annotation called @Parcelize. There is also a way to customize the generated cache.

At the moment of writing these lines, these features are still experimental, so you need to enable them by adding this to the build.gradle:

```
1  androidExtensions {
2      experimental = true
3  }
```

This *experimental* flag means that the API is not final, so it can change in the future.

View cache on a ViewHolder (or any custom classes)

You can now build a cache on any classes in a simple way. The only requisite is that your class implements the LayoutContainer interface. This interface provides the view that the plugin uses to find the subviews. Imagine we have a ViewHolder that is holding a view with the layout described in the previous examples. The required code is:

```
1  class ViewHolder(override val containerView: View)
2          : RecyclerView.ViewHolder(containerView), LayoutContainer {
3
4      fun bind(title: String) {
5          itemTitle.text = "Hello Kotlin!"
6      }
7  }
```

The containerView is the one that we are overriding from the LayoutContainer interface, and that is all you need. From now on, you can access the views directly, no need of prepending itemView to get access to the subviews.

Again, if you check the code generation, you will see that it is taking the view from the cache:

```
1   ((TextView)this._$_findCachedViewById(id.itemTitle))
2       .setText((CharSequence)"Hello Kotlin!");
```

I have used it here on a ViewHolder, but you can see this is generic enough to be used in any classes.

Kotlin Android Extensions to implement Parcelable

With the new @Parcelize annotation, you can effortlessly implement Parcelable. Simply write the annotation, and the plugin does all the hard work:

```
1   @Parcelize
2   class Model(val title: String, val amount: Int) : Parcelable
```

Then, as you may know, you can add the object to an intent:

```
1   val intent = Intent(this, DetailActivity::class.java)
2   intent.putExtra(DetailActivity.EXTRA, model)
3   startActivity(intent)
```

And recover the object from the intent where you need it (in this case, in the target activity):

```
1   val model: Model = intent.getParcelableExtra(EXTRA)
```

Customize the cache build

The last new feature included in this experimental set is a new annotation called @ContainerOptions. This one allows you to customize the way the cache is built, or even prevent a class from creating it.

By default, it uses a Hashmap, as we saw before. This behavior can be changed to use a SparseArray from the Android framework, which may be more efficient under certain situations. Finally, if for some reason you want to disable the cache for a specific class, you also have that option.

Here it is an example of how to change the cache implementation:

```
1  @ContainerOptions(CacheImplementation.SPARSE_ARRAY)
2  class MainActivity : AppCompatActivity() {
3      ...
4  }
```

Currently, the existing options are these:

```
1  public enum class CacheImplementation {
2      SPARSE_ARRAY,
3      HASH_MAP,
4      NO_CACHE;
5
6      ...
7  }
```

Now you know all the features that the Kotlin Android Extensions plugin provides. Now, let's use some of these features in our code.

15.3 Refactoring our code

The modifications we are doing to our sample app to start using Kotlin Android Extensions are fairly simple.

Let's start with MainActivity. We are currently only using a forecast_list view, which is an instance of a RecyclerView. Let's clean up this code.

As said before, we use the id to access the views, so I am changing the id of the RecyclerView so that it does not use underscores, but a more appropriate name for a Kotlin variable. The XML now looks like this:

layout/activity_main.xml

```
1  <FrameLayout
2      xmlns:android="http://schemas.android.com/apk/res/android"
3      android:layout_width="match_parent"
4      android:layout_height="match_parent">
5
6      <android.support.v7.widget.RecyclerView
7          android:id="@+id/forecastList"
8          android:layout_width="match_parent"
9          android:layout_height="match_parent"/>
10
11 </FrameLayout>
```

And now we can just get rid of the find line. Start writing the id of the view, and the autocomplete should help you add the import. Otherwise, you will need to add this:

ui/activities/MainActivity.kt

```
1  import kotlinx.android.synthetic.main.activity_main.*
```

This is the resulting code:

ui/activities/MainActivity.kt

```
1  override fun onCreate(savedInstanceState: Bundle?) {
2      super.onCreate(savedInstanceState)
3      setContentView(R.layout.activity_main)
4
5      forecastList.layoutManager = LinearLayoutManager(this)
6      ...
7  }
```

There is not much improvement because this layout only had one view. But the ForecastListAdapter can also benefit from the use of this plugin. Here, we can use the mechanism to bind the properties into a view, which will help us to remove all the find code inside the ViewHolder.

This is the synthetic import you will need for item_forecast:

ui/adapters/ForecastListAdapter.kt

```
1   import kotlinx.android.synthetic.main.item_forecast.view.*
```

Now we can find the views from `itemView` property inside the `ViewHolder`. As I mentioned before, you can use those properties over any other views, but it will crash if the view does not contain the requested sub-views.

There is no need to declare properties for the views anymore, you can use them directly:

ui/adapters/ForecastListAdapter.kt

```
1   class ViewHolder(view: View, val itemClick: (Forecast) -> Unit) :
2           RecyclerView.ViewHolder(view) {
3
4       fun bindForecast(forecast: Forecast) {
5           with(forecast) {
6               Picasso.with(itemView.ctx).load(iconUrl).into(itemView.icon)
7               itemView.date.text = date
8               itemView.description.text = description
9               itemView.maxTemperature.text = "$high"
10              itemView.minTemperature.text = "$low"
11              itemView.setOnItemClickListener { itemClick(this) }
12          }
13      }
14  }
```

Our layout is pretty simple, and it will not affect performance. In any case, remember what we talked in the section above: this is not caching the views, which implies that each call to the bind function is doing `findViewById` under the hood for all its views.

To solve it, you can use the new features in Kotlin 1.1.4. First, enable the *experimental* flag in the `build.gradle`:

app/build.gradle

```
1  androidExtensions {
2      experimental = true
3  }
```

Now update the `ViewHolder`. You will not need to access the views through the `itemView` anymore, as now the views behave as `ViewHolder` properties. Check that the import is different too:

ui/adapters/ForecastListAdapter.kt

```
1  import kotlinx.android.synthetic.main.item_forecast.*
2
3  class ForecastListAdapter(private val weekForecast: ForecastList,
4          private val itemClick: (Forecast) -> Unit) :
5          RecyclerView.Adapter<ForecastListAdapter.ViewHolder>() {
6
7      ...
8
9      class ViewHolder(override val containerView: View,
10             private val itemClick: (Forecast) -> Unit)
11         : RecyclerView.ViewHolder(containerView), LayoutContainer {
12
13         fun bindForecast(forecast: Forecast) {
14             with(forecast) {
15                 Picasso.with(itemView.ctx).load(iconUrl).into(icon)
16                 dateText.text = date
17                 descriptionText.text = description
18                 maxTemperature.text = "${high}º"
19                 minTemperature.text = "${low}º"
20                 itemView.setOnClickListener { itemClick(this) }
21             }
22         }
23     }
24  }
```

I did a change in the XML too, so that the names of the views are different from the properties in `Forecast`. Otherwise you will have issues to refer to them:

layout/item_forecast.xml

```
1   <TextView
2       android:id="@+id/dateText"
3       android:layout_width="match_parent"
4       android:layout_height="wrap_content"
5       android:textAppearance="@style/TextAppearance.AppCompat.Medium"
6       tools:text="May 14, 2015"/>
7
8   <TextView
9       android:id="@+id/descriptionText"
10      android:layout_width="match_parent"
11      android:layout_height="wrap_content"
12      android:textAppearance="@style/TextAppearance.AppCompat.Caption"
13      tools:text="Light Rain"/>
```

Our app is now using Kotlin Android Extensions to find the views. Run it and check that everything is working as expected.

Kotlin Android Extensions plugin helps us reduce some more boilerplate and minimize the code required to access our views. Check the latest changes in the repository[39].

---

[39]https://github.com/antoniolg/Kotlin-for-Android-Developers/tree/chapter-15

16 Application Singleton and Delegated Properties

We are implementing a database soon and if we want to keep our code simple and our app in independent layers (instead of everything added to our activity), we need to have easier access to the application context.

16.1 Application Singleton

The simplest way is to create a singleton the way we would do in Java:

ui/App.kt

```kotlin
class App : Application() {

    companion object {
        private var instance: Application? = null
        fun instance() = instance!!
    }

    override fun onCreate() {
        super.onCreate()
        instance = this
    }
}
```

Remember you need to add this App class to the AndroidManifest.xml in order to be used as the application instance:

AndroidManifest.xml

```
1   <application
2       android:allowBackup="true"
3       android:icon="@mipmap/ic_launcher"
4       android:label="@string/app_name"
5       android:theme="@style/AppTheme"
6       android:name=".ui.App">
7       ...
8   </application>
```

The problem with Android is that we do not have control over many class constructors. For instance, we cannot initialize a non-nullable property, because its value must be declared in the constructor. So we need a nullable variable and then a function that returns a non-nullable value. We know we always have an App instance, and that the first code that executes is application onCreate, so we are safe by assuming instance() function can always return a non-nullable App instance.

However, this solution seems strange. We need to define a property (which already has a getter and a setter) and then a function to return that property. Do we have another way to get a similar result? Yes, we can delegate the value of a property to another class.

16.2 Delegated Properties

There are some typical behaviors we may need in a property that would be interesting to be reused, such as lazy values or observable properties. Instead of having to declare the same code over and over again, Kotlin provides a way to delegate the code that a property needs to another class. These members are known as **delegated properties**.

When we use get or set from a property, the delegate calls to its corresponding getValue and setValue, which can decide if, when and how the value is set or returned.

The structure of a property delegate is:

```
1  class Delegate<T> {
2      operator fun getValue(thisRef: Any?, property: KProperty<*>): T {
3          return ...
4      }
5
6      operator fun setValue(thisRef: Any?, property: KProperty<*>, value: T) {
7          ...
8      }
9  }
```

The T is the type of the property that is delegating its behavior. The getValue function receives a reference to the class and the metadata of the property. The setValue function also receives the assigned value. If the property is immutable (val), it only requires the getValue function.

The snippet below is an example of how the property delegate is assigned:

```
1  class Example {
2    var p: String by Delegate()
3  }
```

It uses **by** reserved word to specify the delegation.

16.3 Standard Delegates

You can find a set of delegates included in the Kotlin standard library. These are the most common circumstances where a delegate may be useful, but we could also create our own.

Lazy

It takes a lambda that runs after the first call to getValue, so the initialization of the property is delayed up to that moment. Subsequent calls return the same value. This delegate is very interesting for things that are not always used or require some other parts to be ready before this one can be declared. We can save memory and skip the initialization until the property is required.

```
1   class App : Application() {
2       val database: SQLiteOpenHelper by lazy {
3           MyDatabaseHelper(applicationContext)
4       }
5
6       override fun onCreate() {
7           super.onCreate()
8           val db = database.writableDatabase
9       }
10  }
```

In this example, the database does not initialize until it is called first time in onCreate. At that moment, we are sure the application context exists and is ready to be used. The lazy operation is thread-safe.

You can also use lazy(LazyThreadSafetyMode.NONE) { ... } if you are not worried about multi-threading and want to get some extra performance.

Observable

This delegate helps us detect changes on any property we need to observe. It executes the declared lambda expression every time the set function is called. So after the new value is assigned, we receive the delegated property, the old value, and the new one.

```
1   class ViewModel(val db: MyDatabase) {
2
3       var myProperty by Delegates.observable("") {
4           _, _, new ->
5           db.saveChanges(this, new)
6       }
7
8   }
```

This example represents some ViewModel class which is aware of myProperty changes and saves them to the database every time a new value is assigned.

Underscores for unused parameters

Since Kotlin 1.1, you can use underscores to avoid giving a name to a lambda argument that you are not using. This simplification helps both the compiler and the reader. The compiler can prevent saving memory for the ignored input arguments, and the reader does not need to parse which parameters are being used and discard the ones that are not.

Vetoable

This delegate is similar to observable, with the difference that it runs before the value is assigned, and lets you decide whether the value must be saved or not. It can be used to check some conditions before saving a value.

```
1   var positiveNumber = Delegates.vetoable(0) {
2       _, _, new ->
3       new >= 0
4   }
```

The former delegate only allows saving the new value if it is a positive number. Inside lambdas, the latest line represents the return value. You cannot use the return word because it will not compile.

lateinit

Sometimes we need something else to initialize a property, but we lack the necessary state available in the constructor, or we are even not able to retrieve it at that point. This second case happens now and then in Android: in activities, fragments, services or broadcast receivers for example. However, a non-abstract property needs a value before the constructor finishes executing. We cannot just wait until we want to assign a value to the property. We have at least a couple of options.

The first one is to use a nullable type and set it to null until we have the real value. With this solution, we then need to check everywhere throughout the code whether the property is null or not. If we are sure that the property will not be null the first time we use it, this may make us write some unnecessary code.

The second alternative is `lateinit`, which can be used to identify that the property should have a non-nullable value, but we are delaying the assignment. If the value is requested before it is assigned, it will throw an exception that identifies the accessed property.

`lateinit` is not exactly a delegate, but a property modifier, and that is why it must be written before the property.

This modifier is helpful in the App singleton example:

```
1   class App : Application() {
2
3       companion object {
4           lateinit var instance: App
5       }
6
7       override fun onCreate() {
8           super.onCreate()
9           instance = this
10      }
11  }
```

`lateinit` is also indispensable when working with a dependency injector such as Dagger, and very useful for tests too.

Values from a map

Another way to delegate the values of a property is to get them from a map, using the name of the property as the key of the map. This delegate lets create an instance of an object from a dynamic map. If we are using immutable properties, the map can be immutable too. For mutable properties, the class requires a `MutableMap` as constructor parameter instead.

Imagine a configuration class we load from a JSON, and assign those keys and values to a map. We could create an instance of a class by passing this map to the constructor:

```
1  class Configuration(map: Map<String, Any?>) {
2      val width: Int by map
3      val height: Int by map
4      val dp: Int by map
5      val deviceName: String by map
6  }
```

As a reference, here it is how we could create the map that this class would require:

```
1  val conf = Configuration(mapOf(
2          "width" to 1080,
3          "height" to 720,
4          "dp" to 240,
5          "deviceName" to "mydevice"
6  ))
```

16.4 How to create a custom delegate

Let's say we want, for instance, to create a non-nullable delegate that can be only assigned once. The second time it is assigned, it will throw an exception.

To define a delegate class, you only need to write a couple of operator functions: getValue and setValue. They have a very specific set of arguments that look like this:

ui/utils/DelegatesExt.kt

```
1  class NotNullSingleValueVar<T> {
2
3      operator fun getValue(thisRef: Any?, property: KProperty<*>): T {
4          return ...
5      }
6
7      operator fun setValue(thisRef: Any?, property: KProperty<*>, value: T) {
8          ...
9      }
10 }
```

This delegate can work with any non-nullable type. It receives a reference of an object of any type, and use T as the type of the getter and the setter. Now we need to implement the methods:

- The getter returns a value if it is assigned; otherwise, it throws an exception.
- The setter assigns the value if it is still null; otherwise, it throws an exception.

ui/utils/DelegatesExt.kt

```
1   class NotNullSingleValueVar<T> {
2
3       private var value: T? = null
4
5       operator fun getValue(thisRef: Any?, property: KProperty<*>): T =
6           value ?: throw IllegalStateException("${property.name} " +
7                   "not initialized")
8       }
9
10      operator fun setValue(thisRef: Any?, property: KProperty<*>, value: T) {
11          this.value = if (this.value == null) value
12          else throw IllegalStateException("${property.name} already initialized")
13      }
14  }
```

Now let's create an object with a function that provides your new delegate:

ui/utils/DelegatesExt.kt

```
1   object DelegatesExt {
2       fun <T> notNullSingleValue() = NotNullSingleValueVar<T>()
3   }
```

This last part is not necessary, but it can help you aggregate all the delegates you implement.

16.5 Reimplementing the App Singleton

Delegates can help us in this situation. We know that our singleton is not going to be null, but we cannot use the constructor to assign the property. So we can make use of a `lateinit` delegate:

ui/App.kt

```
1   class App : Application() {
2
3       companion object {
4           lateinit var instance: App
5       }
6
7       override fun onCreate() {
8           super.onCreate()
9           instance = this
10      }
11  }
```

The problem with this solution is that we could change the value of this instance from anywhere in the app because a var property is required if we want to use lateinit. That is easy to solve by using a private set:

```
1   companion object {
2       lateinit var instance: App
3           private set
4   }
```

Now, the value of the instance can only be modified inside the App class.

But we will make use of our custom delegate instead:

ui/App.kt

```
1   companion object {
2       var instance: App by DelegatesExt.notNullSingleValue()
3   }
```

Though, in this case, lateinit is probably the simplest option, I wanted to show you how to create a custom property delegate and use it in your code.

Take a look at the specific branch of this chapter[40] if you have any doubts.

---

[40]https://github.com/antoniolg/Kotlin-for-Android-Developers/tree/chapter-16

17 Creating an SQLiteOpenHelper

As you may know, Android uses SQLite as a database management system. SQLite is a database embedded into the app, and it is lightweight. That is why it is a good option for mobile apps.

However, the API to work with databases in Android is somewhat raw. You will see you need to write many SQL sentences and map your objects into ContentValues or from Cursors. Thankfully, by using a mix of Kotlin and Anko, we are simplifying this task a lot.

Of course, there are many libraries to work with databases in Android, and all of them work in Kotlin thanks to its interoperability. However, it is possible you can avoid using complicated frameworks if the database is simple, as we are going to see in a minute.

17.1 ManagedSqliteOpenHelper

Anko provides a powerful SqliteOpenHelper which simplifies things a lot. When we use a regular SqliteOpenHelper, we need to call getReadableDatabase() or getWritableDatabase(), and then we can perform our queries over the object we get. After that, we should not forget to call close(). With a ManagedSqliteOpenHelper we just do:

```
1   forecastDbHelper.use {
2   ...
3   }
```

Inside the lambda, we can use SqliteDatabase functions directly. How does it work? Take a look at the implementation of Anko functions; you can learn a good deal of Kotlin from them:

```
1  public fun <T> use(f: SQLiteDatabase.() -> T): T {
2      try {
3          return openDatabase().f()
4      } finally {
5          closeDatabase()
6      }
7  }
```

First, use receives a function and uses it as an extension function for SQLiteDatabase. Thanks to extensions, we can use this inside the braces, and this is referring to the SQLiteDatabase object. This extension function can return a value, so we could do something like this:

```
1  val result = forecastDbHelper.use {
2      val queriedObject = ...
3      queriedObject
4  }
```

Keep in mind that, inside a function, the last line represents the returned value. As T does not have any restrictions, we can return any value. Even Unit if we do not want to return anything.

By using a try-finally, the use function makes sure that the database is closed no matter the extended function succeeds or crashes.

Besides, we have a lot of other handy extension functions over SqliteDatabase that we will use later. For now, let's define the database tables and implement the SqliteOpenHelper.

17.2 Tables definition

Let's create a couple of objects that represent our tables. These objects will be helpful to avoid misspelling table or column names and repetition. We need two tables: one that saves the info of the city, and the other one the forecast for individual days. This second table has a foreign key to the first one.

CityForecastTable first provides the name of the table and then the set of columns it needs: an id (which is the zip code of the city), the name of the city and the country.

data/db/Tables.kt

```
1   object CityForecastTable {
2       const val NAME = "CityForecast"
3       const val ID = "_id"
4       const val CITY = "city"
5       const val COUNTRY = "country"
6   }
```

DayForecast has some more info, so it requires the set of columns you can see below. The last column, cityId, keeps the id of the CityForecast where this forecast belongs.

data/db/Tables.kt

```
1    object DayForecastTable {
2        const val NAME = "DayForecast"
3        const val ID = "_id"
4        const val DATE = "date"
5        const val DESCRIPTION = "description"
6        const val HIGH = "high"
7        const val LOW = "low"
8        const val ICON_URL = "iconUrl"
9        const val CITY_ID = "cityId"
10   }
```

17.3 Implementing SqliteOpenHelper

If you remember, Anko is divided into several libraries to be more lightweight. We already added anko-common, but we also need anko-sqlite if we want to use database features:

app/build.gradle

```
1  dependencies {
2      . . .
3      compile "org.jetbrains.anko:anko-sqlite:$anko_version"
4  }
```

Our `SqliteOpenHelper` will basically manage the creation and upgrade of our database, and will provide the `SqliteDatabase` so that we can work with it. The queries will be extracted to another class:

data/db/ForecastDbHelper.kt

```
1  class ForecastDbHelper() : ManagedSQLiteOpenHelper(App.instance,
2          ForecastDbHelper.DB_NAME, null, ForecastDbHelper.DB_VERSION) {
3      . . .
4  }
```

We are using the `App.instance` we created in the previous chapter, as well as a database name and version. Define these values in the companion object, along with the helper instance:

data/db/ForecastDbHelper.kt

```
1  companion object {
2      const val DB_NAME = "forecast.db"
3      const val DB_VERSION = 1
4      val instance by lazy { ForecastDbHelper() }
5  }
```

The `instance` property uses a `lazy` delegate, which means the object is not created until its first use. That way, if the database is never employed, we avoid creating unnecessary objects. The regular `lazy` delegate is blocking in order to prevent the creation of several instances from different threads. This situation can only happen if two threads try to access the `instance` at the same time, which is difficult but it could happen depending on the type of app you are implementing.

In order to create the database schema, we are required to provide an implementation of the `onCreate` function. When no libraries are used, tables creation is done by writing a raw `CREATE TABLE` query where we define all the columns and their types. However, Anko provides a simple extension function that receives the name of the table and a set of `Pair` objects that identify the name and the type of the column:

data/db/ForecastDbHelper.kt

```
1   db.createTable(CityForecastTable.NAME, true,
2           Pair(CityForecastTable.ID, INTEGER + PRIMARY_KEY),
3           Pair(CityForecastTable.CITY, TEXT),
4           Pair(CityForecastTable.COUNTRY, TEXT))
```

- The first parameter is the name of the table.
- The second parameter, when set to `true`, checks if the table does not exist before trying to create it.
- The third parameter is a `vararg` of `Pairs`. The `vararg` type also exists in Java, and it is a way to pass a variable number of arguments of the same type to a function. The function then receives an array with the objects.

Column types are using a special Anko class called `SqlType`, which can be used together with `SqlTypeModifiers`, such as `PRIMARY_KEY`. The `+` operation is overloaded the same way we saw in chapter 11. This `plus` function properly concatenates both values returning a new special `SqlType`:

```
1   fun SqlType.plus(m: SqlTypeModifier) : SqlType {
2       return SqlTypeImpl(name, if (modifier == null) m.toString()
3               else "$modifier $m")
4   }
```

As you can see, it can also concatenate several modifiers.

Coming back to our code, we can do it better. Kotlin standard library includes a function called `to` which, once more, shows the ability of Kotlin to let us model the language to our needs. It acts as an extension function for the first object and receives another object as a parameter, returning a `Pair` object with them.

```
1   infix fun <A, B> A.to(that: B): Pair<A, B> = Pair(this, that)
```

Functions with one parameter that use the `infix` modifier can be used inline, so the result is quite clean:

```
1  val pair = object1 to object2
```

And this, applied to the creation of our tables:

```
1  db.createTable(CityForecastTable.NAME, true,
2          CityForecastTable.ID to INTEGER + PRIMARY_KEY,
3          CityForecastTable.CITY to TEXT,
4          CityForecastTable.COUNTRY to TEXT)
```

This is how the complete method looks:

data/db/ForecastDbHelper.kt

```
1  override fun onCreate(db: SQLiteDatabase) {
2      db.createTable(CityForecastTable.NAME, true,
3              CityForecastTable.ID to INTEGER + PRIMARY_KEY,
4              CityForecastTable.CITY to TEXT,
5              CityForecastTable.COUNTRY to TEXT)
6
7      db.createTable(DayForecastTable.NAME, true,
8              DayForecastTable.ID to INTEGER + PRIMARY_KEY + AUTOINCREMENT,
9              DayForecastTable.DATE to INTEGER,
10             DayForecastTable.DESCRIPTION to TEXT,
11             DayForecastTable.HIGH to INTEGER,
12             DayForecastTable.LOW to INTEGER,
13             DayForecastTable.ICON_URL to TEXT,
14             DayForecastTable.CITY_ID to INTEGER)
15 }
```

We have a similar function to drop a table. onUpgrade just deletes the tables so that they are recreated. We are using our database just as a cache, so it is the easiest and safest way to be sure the tables are rebuilt as expected. If we had stored persistent data, we would need to improve onUpgrade code by doing the corresponding migration depending on the database version.

```
1  override fun onUpgrade(db: SQLiteDatabase, oldVersion: Int, newVersion: Int) {
2      db.dropTable(CityForecastTable.NAME, true)
3      db.dropTable(DayForecastTable.NAME, true)
4      onCreate(db)
5  }
```

17.4 Dependency injection

Although I am trying not to add much complexity to the code regarding architectures, clean testable code or good practices, I thought it would be a good idea to show another way to simplify our code using Kotlin. If you want to know a little more about topics like dependency inversion or injection, you can check my set of articles about dependency injection in Android using Dagger[41]. The first article covers a light explanation of these terms.

To put it simply, if we want to have classes that are independent one from another, way more testable, and write code that is easy to extend and maintain, we need to make use of dependency inversion. Instead of instantiating the collaborators inside the class, we provide them (usually via constructor) and instantiate them somewhere else. That way, we can substitute them by other objects that, for instance, implement the same interface, or make use of mocks in tests.

However, now those dependencies must be provided from somewhere, so the dependency injection consists of providing the collaborators required by the classes. Developers usually delegate this task to a dependency injector. Dagger[42] is probably the most famous dependency injector for Android. It is, of course, an excellent alternative when we need some complexity to provide those dependencies.

But a simpler alternative is to make use of default values in constructors. We can provide the dependency by assigning a default value to constructor arguments, and then provide a different instance if we need it in other situations. For example, in our ForecastDbHelper we can provide the context in a smarter way:

---

[41]http://antonioleiva.com/dependency-injection-android-dagger-part-1/
[42]https://google.github.io/dagger/

```
1   class ForecastDbHelper(ctx: Context = App.instance) :
2       ManagedSQLiteOpenHelper(ctx, ForecastDbHelper.DB_NAME, null,
3       ForecastDbHelper.DB_VERSION) {
4       ...
5   }
```

Now we have two ways to create this class:

```
1   val dbHelper1 = ForecastDbHelper()    // It will use App.instance
2   val dbHelper2 = ForecastDbHelper(mockedContext) // For tests, for example
```

I will be using this mechanism here and there, so I did not want to continue without explaining the motivation. We already have created the tables, so it is time to start adding and requesting data from them. But before that, I want to talk about collections and functional operations. Remember to check the repository[43] to find the latest changes.

---

[43]https://github.com/antoniolg/Kotlin-for-Android-Developers/tree/chapter-17

18 Collections and functional operations

We have been using collections before in this project, but now it is time to show how powerful they are in combination with functional operations. The good part about functional programming is that instead of explaining how we do things, we just say what we want to do. For instance, if we want to filter a list, instead of creating a list, iterating over the original one and add the items to the new if they satisfy a condition, we simply use a filter function and specify which filter we want to use. That way, we can say a lot more using less code.

Although we can use Java collections, Kotlin provides a good set of native interfaces you will want to use:

- **Iterable**: The parent class. Any classes that inherit from this interface represent a sequence of elements we can iterate over.
- **MutableIterable**: Iterables that support removing items during iteration.
- **Collection**: This class represents a generic collection of elements. We get access to functions that return the size of the collection, whether the collection is empty, contains an item or a set of items. All the methods for this kind of collections are only meant to request data because collections are immutable.
- **MutableCollection**: a `Collection` that supports adding and removing elements. It provides extra functions such as `add`, `remove` or `clear` among others.
- **List**: Probably the most popular collection type. It represents a generic ordered collection of elements. As it is ordered, we can request an item by its position, using the `get` function.
- **MutableList**: a `List` that supports adding and removing elements.
- **Set**: an unordered collection of elements that ignores duplicate elements.
- **MutableSet**: a `Set` that supports adding and removing elements.
- **Map**: a collection of key-value pairs. The keys in a map are unique, which means we cannot have two pairs with the same key in a map.

- **MutableMap**: a Map that supports adding and removing elements.

These collections can apply a set of functional operations. I want to show you a little definition and an example of several operations. It is useful to know what the options are. That way it is easier to identify where these functions can be used.

18.1 Aggregate operations

any

Returns true if at least one element matches the given predicate.

```
1  val list = listOf(1, 2, 3, 4, 5, 6)
2  assertTrue(list.any { it % 2 == 0 })
3  assertFalse(list.any { it > 10 })
```

all

Returns true if all the elements match the given predicate.

```
1  assertTrue(list.all { it < 10 })
2  assertFalse(list.all { it % 2 == 0 })
```

count

Returns the number of elements matching the given predicate.

```
1  assertEquals(3, list.count { it % 2 == 0 })
```

fold

Accumulates the value starting with an initial value and applying an operation from the first to the last element in a collection.

```
1  assertEquals(25, list.fold(4) { total, next -> total + next })
```

foldRight

Same as fold, but it goes from the last element to first.

```
1  assertEquals(25, list.foldRight(4) { total, next -> total + next })
```

forEach

Performs the given operation to each element.

```
1  list.forEach { println(it) }
```

forEachIndexed

Same as forEach, though we also get the index of the element.

```
1  list.forEachIndexed { index, value
2         -> println("position $index contains a $value") }
```

max

Returns the largest element or null if there are no elements.

```
1  assertEquals(6, list.max())
```

maxBy

Returns the first element yielding the largest value of the given function or null if there are no elements.

```
1   // The element whose negative is greater
2   assertEquals(1, list.maxBy { -it })
```

min

Returns the smallest element or null if there are no elements.

```
1   assertEquals(1, list.min())
```

minBy

Returns the first element yielding the smallest value of the given function or null if there are no elements.

```
1   // The element whose negative is smaller
2   assertEquals(6, list.minBy { -it })
```

none

Returns true if no elements match the given predicate.

```
1   // No elements are divisible by 7
2   assertTrue(list.none { it % 7 == 0 })
```

reduce

Same as fold, but it does not use an initial value. It accumulates the value applying an operation from the first to the last element in a collection.

```
1   assertEquals(21, list.reduce { total, next -> total + next })
```

reduceRight

Same as reduce, but it goes from the last element to first.

```
1   assertEquals(21, list.reduceRight { total, next -> total + next })
```

sumBy

Returns the sum of all values produced by the transform function from the elements in the collection.

```
1   assertEquals(3, list.sumBy { it % 2 })
```

18.2 Filtering operations

drop

Returns a list containing all elements except first n elements.

```
1   assertEquals(listOf(5, 6), list.drop(4))
```

dropWhile

Returns a list containing all elements except first elements that satisfy the given predicate.

```
1   assertEquals(listOf(3, 4, 5, 6), list.dropWhile { it < 3 })
```

dropLastWhile

Returns a list containing all elements except last elements that satisfy the given predicate.

```
1   assertEquals(listOf(1, 2, 3, 4), list.dropLastWhile { it > 4 })
```

filter

Returns a list containing all elements matching the given predicate.

```
1   assertEquals(listOf(2, 4, 6), list.filter { it % 2 == 0 })
```

filterNot

Returns a list containing all elements not matching the given predicate.

```
1   assertEquals(listOf(1, 3, 5), list.filterNot { it % 2 == 0 })
```

filterNotNull

Returns a list containing all elements that are not null.

```
1   val listWithNull = listOf(1, null, 2, 3, null, 4)
2   assertEquals(listOf(1, 2, 3, 4), listWithNull.filterNotNull())
```

slice

Returns a list containing elements at specified indices.

```
1   assertEquals(listOf(2, 4, 5), list.slice(listOf(1, 3, 4)))
```

take

Returns a list containing first n elements.

```
1    assertEquals(listOf(1, 2), list.take(2))
```

takeLast

Returns a list containing last n elements.

```
1    assertEquals(listOf(5, 6), list.takeLast(2))
```

takeWhile

Returns a list containing first elements satisfying the given predicate.

```
1    assertEquals(listOf(1, 2), list.takeWhile { it < 3 })
```

18.3 Mapping operations

flatMap

Iterates over the elements creating a new collection for each one, and finally flattens all the collections into a unique list containing all the elements.

```
1    assertEquals(listOf(1, 2, 2, 3, 3, 4, 4, 5, 5, 6, 6, 7),
2            list.flatMap { listOf(it, it + 1) })
```

groupBy

Returns a map of the elements in original collection grouped by the result of given function

```
1   assertEquals(mapOf("odd" to listOf(1, 3, 5), "even" to listOf(2, 4, 6)),
2               list.groupBy { if (it % 2 == 0) "even" else "odd" })
```

map

Returns a list containing the results of applying the given transform function to each element of the original collection.

```
1   assertEquals(listOf(2, 4, 6, 8, 10, 12), list.map { it * 2 })
```

mapIndexed

Returns a list containing the results of applying the given transform function to each element and its index of the original collection.

```
1   assertEquals(listOf (0, 2, 6, 12, 20, 30), list.mapIndexed { index, it
2           -> index * it })
```

mapNotNull

Returns a list containing the results of applying the given transform function to each non-null element of the original collection.

```
1   assertEquals(listOf(2, 4, 6, 8), listWithNull.mapNotNull { it * 2 })
```

18.4 Elements operations

contains

Returns true if the element is found in the collection.

```
1   assertTrue(list.contains(2))
```

elementAt

Returns an element at the given index or throws an IndexOutOfBoundsException if the index is out of bounds of this collection.

```
1   assertEquals(2, list.elementAt(1))
```

elementAtOrElse

Returns an element at the given index or the result of calling the default function if the index is out of bounds of this collection.

```
1   assertEquals(20, list.elementAtOrElse(10, { 2 * it }))
```

elementAtOrNull

Returns an element at the given index or null if the index is out of bounds of this collection.

```
1   assertNull(list.elementAtOrNull(10))
```

first

Returns the first element matching the given predicate. It will throw a NoSuchElementException if no elements are found.

```
1   assertEquals(2, list.first { it % 2 == 0 })
```

firstOrNull

Returns the first element matching the given predicate, or null if no element was found.

```
1   assertNull(list.firstOrNull { it % 7 == 0 })
```

indexOf

Returns the first index of the element, or -1 if the collection does not contain the element.

```
1   assertEquals(3, list.indexOf(4))
```

indexOfFirst

Returns index of the first element matching the given predicate, or -1 if the collection does not contain such element.

```
1   assertEquals(1, list.indexOfFirst { it % 2 == 0 })
```

indexOfLast

Returns index of the last element matching the given predicate, or -1 if the collection does not contain such element.

```
1   assertEquals(5, list.indexOfLast { it % 2 == 0 })
```

last

Returns the last element matching the given predicate. It throws a NoSuchElementException if no elements are found.

```
1   assertEquals(6, list.last { it % 2 == 0 })
```

lastIndexOf

Returns the last index of the element, or -1 if the collection does not contain the element.

```
1   val listRepeated = listOf(2, 2, 3, 4, 5, 5, 6)
2   assertEquals(5, listRepeated.lastIndexOf(5))
```

lastOrNull

Returns the last element matching the given predicate, or `null` if no such element was found.

```
1   val list = listOf(1, 2, 3, 4, 5, 6)
2   assertNull(list.lastOrNull { it % 7 == 0 })
```

single

Returns the single element matching the given predicate, or throws an exception if there is no or more than one matching element.

```
1   assertEquals(5, list.single { it % 5 == 0 })
```

singleOrNull

Returns the single element matching the given predicate, or `null` if the element was not found or more than one element was found.

```
1   assertNull(list.singleOrNull { it % 7 == 0 })
```

18.5 Generation operations

merge

Returns a list of values built from elements of both collections with same indexes using the provided transform function. The list has the length of the shortest collection.

```
1    val list = listOf(1, 2, 3, 4, 5, 6)
2    val listRepeated = listOf(2, 2, 3, 4, 5, 5, 6)
3    assertEquals(listOf(3, 4, 6, 8, 10, 11), list.merge(listRepeated) { it1, it2 ->
4            it1 + it2 })
```

partition

Splits original collection into a pair of collections, where the first collection contains elements for which the predicate returned true, while the second collection contains elements for which the predicate returned false.

```
1    assertEquals(Pair(listOf(2, 4, 6), listOf(1, 3, 5)),
2            list.partition { it % 2 == 0 })
```

plus

Returns a list containing all elements of the original collection and then all elements of the given collection. Because of the name of the function, we can use the '+' operator with it.

```
1    assertEquals(listOf(1, 2, 3, 4, 5, 6, 7, 8), list + listOf(7, 8))
```

zip

Returns a list of pairs built from the elements of both collections with the same indexes. The list has the length of the shortest collection.

```
1    assertEquals(listOf(Pair(1, 7), Pair(2, 8)), list.zip(listOf(7, 8)))
```

unzip

Generates a Pair of Lists from a List of Pairs

```
1    assertEquals(Pair(listOf(5, 6), listOf(7, 8)), listOf(Pair(5, 7), Pair(6, 8)).unzip())
```

18.6 Ordering operations

reverse

Returns a list with elements in reversed order.

```
1    val unsortedList = listOf(3, 2, 7, 5)
2    assertEquals(listOf(5, 7, 2, 3), unsortedList.reverse())
```

sort

Returns a sorted list of all elements.

```
1    assertEquals(listOf(2, 3, 5, 7), unsortedList.sort())
```

sortBy

Returns a list of all elements, sorted by the specified comparator.

```
1    assertEquals(listOf(3, 7, 2, 5), unsortedList.sortBy { it % 3 })
```

sortDescending

Returns a sorted list of all elements, in descending order.

```
1    assertEquals(listOf(7, 5, 3, 2), unsortedList.sortDescending())
```

sortDescendingBy

Returns a sorted list of all elements, in descending order by the results of the specified
order function.

```
1   assertEquals(listOf(2, 5, 7, 3), unsortedList.sortDescendingBy { it % 3 })
```

19 Saving and requesting data from the database

A previous chapter covered the creation of an SQLiteOpenHelper, but now we need a way to use it to persist our data into the database and recover it when necessary. Another class, called ForecastDb, is making use of it.

19.1 Creating database model classes

First, we are going to create the model classes for the database. Do you remember the map delegates we saw? We are using them to map those fields directly to the database and vice-versa.

Let's take a look at the CityForecast class first:

data/db/DbClasses.kt

```kotlin
class CityForecast(val map: MutableMap<String, Any?>,
                        val dailyForecast: List<DayForecast>) {
    var _id: Long by map
    var city: String by map
    var country: String by map

    constructor(id: Long, city: String, country: String,
                dailyForecast: List<DayForecast>)
    : this(HashMap(), dailyForecast) {
        this._id = id
        this.city = city
        this.country = country
    }
}
```

The default constructor is getting a map, presumably filled with the values of the properties, and a dailyForecast. Thanks to the delegates, the values are mapped to the corresponding properties based on the name of the key. If we want to make the mapping work correctly, the names of the properties must be the same as the names of the columns in the database. We will see why later.

Besides, a second constructor is necessary. This is because we are mapping classes from the domain back to the database. So instead of using a map, extracting the values from the properties is more convenient. We pass an empty map, but again, thanks to the delegate, when we set a value to a property, it automatically adds a new value to the map. That way, we have our map ready to be added to the database. After writing some extra code, you will see that it works like magic.

Now we need a second class, DayForecast, which corresponds to the second table. This one has one property per column, and also uses a secondary constructor. The only difference is that we are not assigning an id because this one is auto-generated by SQLite.

data/db/DbClasses.kt

```
1   class DayForecast(var map: MutableMap<String, Any?>) {
2       var _id: Long by map
3       var date: Long by map
4       var description: String by map
5       var high: Int by map
6       var low: Int by map
7       var iconUrl: String by map
8       var cityId: Long by map
9
10      constructor(date: Long, description: String, high: Int, low: Int,
11                  iconUrl: String, cityId: Long) : this(HashMap()) {
12          this.date = date
13          this.description = description
14          this.high = high
15          this.low = low
16          this.iconUrl = iconUrl
17          this.cityId = cityId
18      }
19  }
```

These classes helps us map the data between objects and SQLite tables, in both directions.

19.2 Writing and requesting data

The `SqliteOpenHelper` is just the tool, the channel between object-oriented and SQL worlds. We are using it in a new class, to request data already saved in the database, and to save fresh data. The definition of the class is using a `ForecastDbHelper` and a `DataMapper` that converts classes from database to domain models. I am still using default values as an easy way of dependency injection:

data/db/ForecastDb.kt

```
1   class ForecastDb(
2       private val forecastDbHelper: ForecastDbHelper = ForecastDbHelper.instance,
3       private val dataMapper: DbDataMapper = DbDataMapper()) {
4           ...
5   }
```

Both functions will call `use()`, the function we saw in the previous chapter. The value that the lambda returns will be used as the result of our function. So let's define a function that requests a forecast based on a zip code and a date:

data/db/ForecastDb.kt

```
1   fun requestForecastByZipCode(zipCode: Long, date: Long) = forecastDbHelper.use {
2       ....
3   }
```

Not much to explain here: we return the result of the `use` function as the result of our function.

Requesting a forecast

The first request that needs to be done is the daily forecast, because we need the list to create the city object. Anko provides a simple request builder, so let's take advantage of it:

data/db/ForecastDb.kt

```
1   val dailyRequest = "${DayForecastTable.CITY_ID} = ? " +
2       "AND ${DayForecastTable.DATE} >= ?"
3
4   val dailyForecast = select(DayForecastTable.NAME)
5           .whereSimple(dailyRequest, zipCode.toString(), date.toString())
6           .parseList { DayForecast(HashMap(it)) }
```

The first line, dailyRequest, is the where part of the query. This is the first parameter the whereSimple function needs, and it is very similar to what we would do in regular use of the helper. There is another function called simply where, which takes some tags and values and match them. I do not find it very useful because I think it adds more boilerplate, though it has the advantage of parsing the values to the Strings we need. The following snippet shows how it would look with it:

data/db/ForecastDb.kt

```
1   val dailyRequest = "${DayForecastTable.CITY_ID} = {id}" +
2   "AND ${DayForecastTable.DATE} >= {date}"
3
4   val dailyForecast = select(DayForecastTable.NAME)
5           .where(dailyRequest, "id" to zipCode, "date" to date)
6           .parseList { DayForecast(HashMap(it)) }
```

You can choose your preferred one. The select function is simple, it just asks for the name of the table. The parse methods are where the magic happens. In this case, we are using the function parseList, which assumes we are requesting a list of items. It uses a RowParser or MapRowParser to convert the cursor into a list of object. The difference between both is that the RowParser relies on the order of the columns, while the MapRowParser uses the name of the column as the key of the map.

These two overloads conflict between them, so we cannot directly use the simplification that prevents from the need of creating an object explicitly. T This conflict can be solved by implementing an extension function. I am creating a function that receives a lambda and returns a MapRowParser. The parser will use that lambda to create the object:

extensions/DatabaseExtensions.kt

```
1   fun <T : Any> SelectQueryBuilder.parseList(
2       parser: (Map<String, Any?>) -> T): List<T> =
3           parseList(object : MapRowParser<T> {
4               override fun parseRow(columns: Map<String, Any?>): T = parser(columns)
5           })
```

If you do not fully understand it yet, you can come back once we dive deep into generics. The previous function helps simplify the parseList request to:

```
1   parseList { DayForecast(HashMap(it)) }
```

The immutable map that the parser receives is converted into a mutable map (we need it to be mutable in our database model) by using the corresponding constructor from the HashMap. This HashMap is used by the constructor of DayForecast.

So, to understand what is happening behind the scenes, the request returns a Cursor. parseList iterates over it and gets the rows from the Cursor until it reaches the last one. For each row, it creates a map with the columns as keys and assigns the value to the corresponding key. The map is then returned to the parser.

If there are no results for the request, parseList returns an empty list.

Next step will request the city in a similar way:

data/db/ForecastDb.kt

```
1   val city = select(CityForecastTable.NAME)
2           .whereSimple("${CityForecastTable.ID} = ?", zipCode.toString())
3           .parseOpt { CityForecast(HashMap(it), dailyForecast) }
```

The difference here: we are using parseOpt instead. This function returns a nullable object. The result can be null or a single object, depending on whether the request finds something in the database or not. There is another function called parseSingle, which does essentially the same but returns a non-nullable object. So if it does not find a row in the database, it throws an exception. In our case, the first time we query a city, it will not be there, so using parseOpt is safer. I also created a handy function to prevent the need for object creation:

extensions/DatabaseExtensions.kt

```
1   fun <T : Any> SelectQueryBuilder.parseOpt(
2       parser: (Map<String, Any?>) -> T): T? =
3           parseOpt(object : MapRowParser<T> {
4               override fun parseRow(columns: Map<String, Any?>): T = parser(columns)
5           })
```

Finally, if the returned city is not null, we convert it to a domain object and return it, using the dataMapper. Otherwise, we just return null. As you may remember, last line inside a lambda represents what the lambda returns. So it will return an object from the type CityForecast?:

data/db/ForecastDb.kt

```
1   if (city != null) dataMapper.convertToDomain(city) else null
```

DataMapper function is easy:

data/db/DbDataMapper.kt

```
1   fun convertToDomain(forecast: CityForecast) = with(forecast) {
2       val daily = dailyForecast.map { convertDayToDomain(it) }
3       ForecastList(_id, city, country, daily)
4   }
5
6   private fun convertDayToDomain(dayForecast: DayForecast) = with(dayForecast) {
7       Forecast(date, description, high, low, iconUrl)
8   }
```

So this is how the complete function looks like:

data/db/ForecastDb.kt

```
1  fun requestForecastByZipCode(zipCode: Long, date: Long) = forecastDbHelper.use {
2
3      val dailyRequest = "${DayForecastTable.CITY_ID} = ? AND " +
4          "${DayForecastTable.DATE} >= ?"
5      val dailyForecast = select(DayForecastTable.NAME)
6              .whereSimple(dailyRequest, zipCode.toString(), date.toString())
7              .parseList { DayForecast(HashMap(it)) }
8
9      val city = select(CityForecastTable.NAME)
10             .whereSimple("${CityForecastTable.ID} = ?", zipCode.toString())
11             .parseOpt { CityForecast(HashMap(it), dailyForecast) }
12
13     if (city != null) dataMapper.convertToDomain(city) else null
14 }
```

Another interesting functionality from Anko I am not showing here is that you can make use of a `classParser()` instead of the `MapRowParser` we are using, which uses reflection to fill a class based on the names of the columns. I prefer the other way because we do not need reflection and have more control over the transformations, but it can be of use for you at some point.

Saving a forecast

The `saveForecast` function clears the data from the database so that we save fresh data, converts the domain forecast model to database model, and inserts each daily forecast and the city forecast. The structure is similar to the previous one: it returns the value from the use function from the database helper. In this case, we do not need a result, so it will return `Unit`.

data/db/ForecastDb.kt

```
1  fun saveForecast(forecast: ForecastList) = forecastDbHelper.use {
2      ...
3  }
```

First, we clear both tables. Anko does not provide any beautiful way to do it, so we are creating an extension function for `SQLiteDatabase` that executes the proper SQL query for us:

extensions/DatabaseExtensions.kt

```
1   fun SQLiteDatabase.clear(tableName: String) {
2       execSQL("delete from $tableName")
3   }
```

The function is applied to both tables:

data/db/ForecastDb.kt

```
1   clear(CityForecastTable.NAME)
2   clear(DayForecastTable.NAME)
```

Now it is time to convert the data, and use the result to execute the insert queries.
The with function may help us:

data/db/ForecastDb.kt

```
1   with(dataMapper.convertFromDomain(forecast)) {
2       . . .
3   }
```

The conversion from the domain model is straightforward too:

data/db/DbDataMapper.kt

```
1   fun convertFromDomain(forecast: ForecastList) = with(forecast) {
2       val daily = dailyForecast.map { convertDayFromDomain(id, it) }
3       CityForecast(id, city, country, daily)
4   }
5
6   private fun convertDayFromDomain(cityId: Long, forecast: Forecast) =
7       with(forecast) {
8           DayForecast(date, description, high, low, iconUrl, cityId)
9   }
```

Inside the block, we can use dailyForecast and map without the need of referring to a
variable, just like if we were inside the class. We are using another Anko function for
the insertion, which asks for a table name and a vararg of Pair<String, Any>. The
function will convert the vararg to the ContentValues object the Android SDK needs.
So our task consists of transforming the map into a vararg array. We are creating
another extension function for Map to do that:

extensions/CollectionExtensions.kt

```
1   fun <K, V : Any> MutableMap<K, V?>.toVarargArray():
2       Array<out Pair<K, V>> = map { Pair(it.key, it.value!!) }.toTypedArray()
```

It works over a Map with nullable values (this was a condition from the map delegate) and converts it to an Array with non-nullable values (select function requisite) of pairs. Another complex one you do not need to understand yet. I will be covering nullity soon.

So, with this new function we can do:

data/db/ForecastDb.kt

```
1   insert(CityForecastTable.NAME, *map.toVarargArray())
```

It inserts a new row in the CityForecast table. The '*' used before the result of toVarargArray indicates that the array is decomposed to a vararg parameter. This is done automatically in Java, but we need to make it explicit in Kotlin.

And the same for each daily forecast:

data/db/ForecastDb.kt

```
1   dailyForecast.forEach { insert(DayForecastTable.NAME, *it.map.toVarargArray()) }
```

So, with the use of maps, we have been able to convert classes to database registers and vice-versa in an effortless way. Once we have these extension functions ready, we can use them for other projects, so it is a well-paid effort.

The complete code of this function:

data/db/ForecastDb.kt

```
1   fun saveForecast(forecast: ForecastList) = forecastDbHelper.use {
2
3       clear(CityForecastTable.NAME)
4       clear(DayForecastTable.NAME)
5
6       with(dataMapper.convertFromDomain(forecast)) {
7           insert(CityForecastTable.NAME, *map.toVarargArray())
8           dailyForecast forEach {
9               insert(DayForecastTable.NAME, *it.map.toVarargArray())
10          }
11      }
12  }
```

Much new code was involved in this chapter, so you can take a look at the repository[44] to review it.

[44]https://github.com/antoniolg/Kotlin-for-Android-Developers/tree/chapter-19

20 Null safety in Kotlin

Null-safety is one of the most exciting features in Kotlin when you come from Java 7. However, as you have seen during this book, it is so implicit in the language we hardly had to worry about it until the previous chapter.

Being `null` considered the billion-dollar mistake by its creator[45], it is true that we sometimes need to define whether a variable contains a value or not. In Java, though annotations and IDEs are helping a lot these days, we can still do something like:

```
1   Forecast forecast = null;
2   forecast.toString();
```

This code compiles correctly (you may get a warning from the IDE), and when it runs, it naturally throws a `NullPointerException`. This is unsafe, and even if you think that you could be able to have everything under control, as the code grows you will start losing track of the things that could be null. So we end up with lots of `NullPointerExceptions` or lots of nullity checks (probably a mix of both).

20.1 How Null types work

Most modern languages solve this issue in some way. Kotlin, the same as other similar languages such as Swift, **make use of question marks to identify nullable types**. That way, if a variable can be null, the compiler forces to deal with it in some way.

As everything is an object in Kotlin (even Java primitive types), everything can be null. So, of course, we can have a nullable integer:

```
1   val a: Int? = null
```

You cannot work directly with a nullable type without doing some checks before. This code does not compile:

---

[45]https://en.wikipedia.org/wiki/Tony_Hoare

```
1   val a: Int? = null
2   a.toLong()
```

That variable could be null and **the compiler is aware of that**, so until the nullity is checked, you cannot use it.

Here it is when another feature of the Kotlin compiler comes into action: the smart cast. If we check the nullity of an object, from that moment the object is automatically cast to its non-nullable type. Let's see an example:

```
1   val a: Int? = null
2   ...
3   if (a != null) {
4       a.toLong()
5   }
```

Inside the if, a becomes Int instead of Int?, so we can use it without checking nullity anymore or doing any castings. The code outside the if context, of course, has to deal with it.

This smart cast only works if a variable cannot be concurrently modified because otherwise the value could have been changed from another thread, and the previous check would be false at that moment. The compiler supports smart casting for val properties or local (val or var) variables.

This can sound like much work. Do we have to fill all our code with nullity checks? Of course not. First, because most of the time you will not need null objects. Null references are more unused that one could think, you will realize when you start figuring out whether a variable should be null or not. But Kotlin also has some operators to do this task easier. We can, for instance, simplify the previous code to:

```
1   val a: Int? = null
2   ...
3   a?.toLong()
```

Here we are using the **safe call operator (?.)**. The previous line is only executed if the variable is not null. Otherwise, it does nothing. Also, we can even provide an alternative for the null case using the **Elvis operator (?:)**:

```
1   val a: Int? = null
2   ...
3   val myLong = a?.toLong() ?: 0L
```

Since `throw` and `return` are also expressions in Kotlin, they can be used in the right side of the Elvis operator:

```
1   val myLong = a?.toLong() ?: return false
```

```
1   val myLong = a?.toLong() ?: throw IllegalStateException()
```

However, there may be situations when we know for sure we are dealing with a non-nullable variable, but the type is nullable. We can force the compiler to deal with nullable types skipping the restriction by using the **!! operator**:

```
1   val a: Int? = null
2   a!!.toLong()
```

The previous code compiles, but it will crash. So we must make sure we only use it in a reduced number of situations. Usually, we can choose alternative solutions. A code full of !! is a smell, because it brings back the possible exceptions we are trying to avoid with nullable types.

20.2 Nullity and Java libraries

Ok, so the previous explanation works perfectly well with Kotlin code. But what happens with Java libraries in general, and Android SDK in particular? In Java, every object can be null by definition. So we would have to deal with a lot potentially null variables which in real life are never null. This means our code could end up with hundreds of !! operators, which is not a good idea at all.

When you are dealing with the Android SDK, you will probably see that some arguments are marked with a single '!' when a Java method is used. For instance, something that gets an `Object` in Java is represented as `Any!` in Kotlin. This special operator represents that it is up to the developer to decide whether that variable should be null or not.

Luckily, latest versions of the Android framework and the support library are starting using the @Nullable and @NonNull annotations to identify the parameters that can be null or the functions that can return null, and the Kotlin compiler can detect that and choose the appropriate translation into Kotlin language.

Said that, if we are for instance overriding onCreate for an Activity, we need to mark savedInstanceState as nullable:

```
1   override fun onCreate(savedInstanceState: Bundle?) {
2   }
```

Otherwise it will show an error. We cannot use this implementation:

```
1   override fun onCreate(savedInstanceState: Bundle) {
2   }
```

This is great because an activity can receive a null bundle, and we get the right implementation for free. However, there are parts of the SDK that are missing annotations yet. So when in doubt, you can just use a nullable object and deal with the possible null. Remember, if you use !! it is because you are sure that the object cannot be null, so you can declare it as non-nullable directly.

21 Creating the business logic to data access

After implementing the access to the server and a way to interact with the database, it is time to put things together. The logical steps would be:

1. Request the required data from the database
2. Check if there is data for the corresponding week
3. If it finds the required data, it is returned so that the UI can render it
4. Otherwise, it requests the data to the server
5. The result is saved in the database and returned so that the UI can render it

Our commands should not need to deal with all this logic. The source of the data is an implementation detail that could easily require a logic modification, so adding some extra code that abstracts the commands from the access to the data sounds like a good idea. In our implementation, it will iterate over a list of sources until it finds a proper result.

So let's start by specifying the interface any data source that wants to be used by our provider should implement:

```
1  interface ForecastDataSource {
2      fun requestForecastByZipCode(zipCode: Long, date: Long): ForecastList?
3  }
```

The provider requires a function that receives a zip code and a date, and it should return a weekly forecast from that day.

domain/datasource/ForecastProvider.kt

```
1   class ForecastProvider(private val sources: List<ForecastDataSource> =
2           ForecastProvider.SOURCES) {
3
4       companion object {
5           const val DAY_IN_MILLIS = 1000 * 60 * 60 * 24
6           val SOURCES = listOf(ForecastDb(), ForecastServer())
7       }
8   ...
9   }
```

The forecast provider receives a list of sources, that once again can be specified through the constructor (for test purposes for instance), but I am defaulting it to a SOURCES list defined in the companion object. It will use a database source and a server source. The order is essential, because it will iterate over the sources, and the search will be stopped when any of the sources returns a valid result. The logical order is to search first locally (in the database) and then through the API.

So the main method looks like this:

domain/datasource/ForecastProvider.kt

```
1   fun requestByZipCode(zipCode: Long, days: Int): ForecastList
2               = sources.firstResult { requestSource(it, days, zipCode) }
```

It gets the first result that is not null. When searching through the list of functional operators explained in chapter 18, I could not find one that did exactly what I was looking for. So, as we have access to Kotlin sources, I just copied first function and modified it to behave as expected:

extensions/CollectionsExtensions.kt

```
1   inline fun <T, R : Any> Iterable<T>.firstResult(predicate: (T) -> R?): R {
2       for (element in this) {
3           val result = predicate(element)
4           if (result != null) return result
5       }
6       throw NoSuchElementException("No element matching predicate was found.")
7   }
```

The function receives a predicate which gets an object of type T and returns a value of type R?. The generic type specifies that the predicate can return null, but our firstResult function cannot. That is the reason why it returns a value of type R.

How does it work? It iterates and executes the predicate over the elements in the Iterable collection. When the result of the predicate is not null, this result is returned.

If we wanted to include the case where all the sources can return null, we could have derived from firstOrNull function instead. The difference would consist of returning null instead of throwing an exception in the last line. But I am not dealing with those details in this code.

In our example T = ForecastDataSource and R = ForecastList. But remember the function specified in ForecastDataSource returned a ForecastList?, which equals R?, so everything matches perfectly. The function requestSource just makes the previous function look more readable:

domain/datasource/ForecastProvider.kt

```
1   fun requestSource(source: ForecastDataSource, days: Int, zipCode: Long):
2           ForecastList? {
3       val res = source.requestForecastByZipCode(zipCode, todayTimeSpan())
4       return if (res != null && res.size() >= days) res else null
5   }
```

The request is executed and only returns a value if the result is not null and the number of days matches the parameter. Otherwise, the source does not have enough up-to-date data to return a successful result.

The function todayTimeSpan() calculates the time in milliseconds for the current day, eliminating the "time" offset, and keeping only the day. Some of the sources (in our case the database) may need it. The server defaults to today unless we specify it, so it will be ignored there.

domain/datasource/ForecastProvider.kt

```
1  private fun todayTimeSpan() = System.currentTimeMillis() /
2      DAY_IN_MILLIS * DAY_IN_MILLIS
```

The complete code of this class would be:

domain/datasource/ForecastProvider.kt

```
1  class ForecastProvider(private val sources: List<ForecastDataSource> =
2          ForecastProvider.SOURCES) {
3
4      companion object {
5          const val DAY_IN_MILLIS = 1000 * 60 * 60 * 24;
6          val SOURCES = listOf(ForecastDb(), ForecastServer())
7      }
8
9      fun requestByZipCode(zipCode: Long, days: Int): ForecastList
10             = sources.firstResult { requestSource(it, days, zipCode) }
11
12     private fun requestSource(source: RepositorySource, days: Int,
13             zipCode: Long): ForecastList? {
14         val res = source.requestForecastByZipCode(zipCode, todayTimeSpan())
15         return if (res != null && res.size >= days) res else null
16     }
17
18     private fun todayTimeSpan() = System.currentTimeMillis() /
19             DAY_IN_MILLIS * DAY_IN_MILLIS
20 }
```

We already defined ForecastDb. It just now needs to implement ForecastDataSource:

data/db/ForecastDb.kt

```
1  class ForecastDb(private val forecastDbHelper: ForecastDbHelper =
2          ForecastDbHelper.instance,
3          private val dataMapper: DbDataMapper = DbDataMapper())
4          : ForecastDataSource {
5
6      override fun requestForecastByZipCode(zipCode: Long, date: Long) =
7              forecastDbHelper.use {
8          ...
9          }
10         ...
11 }
```

We have not implemented `ForecastServer` yet, but it is straightforward. It makes use of a `ForecastDb` to save the response once it is received from the server. That way, we can keep it cached into the database for future requests.

data/server/ForecastServer.kt

```
1  class ForecastServer(
2      private val dataMapper: ServerDataMapper = ServerDataMapper(),
3      private val forecastDb: ForecastDb = ForecastDb())
4      : ForecastDataSource {
5
6      override fun requestForecastByZipCode(zipCode: Long, date: Long):
7              ForecastList? {
8          val result = ForecastByZipCodeRequest(zipCode).execute()
9          val converted = dataMapper.convertToDomain(zipCode, result)
10         forecastDb.saveForecast(converted)
11         return forecastDb.requestForecastByZipCode(zipCode, date)
12     }
13
14 }
```

It also makes use of a data mapper, the first one we created, though I modified the name of some methods to make it similar to the data mapper we used for the database model. You can take a look at the provider to see the details.

The overridden function makes the request to the server, converts the result to domain objects and saves them into the database. It finally returns the values from the database, because we need the row ids that were self-generated by the insert query.

With these last steps, the provider is already implemented. Now we need to start using it. The ForecastCommand no longer should interact directly with server requests, nor convert the data to the domain model.

domain/commands/RequestForecastCommand.kt

```kotlin
1  class RequestForecastCommand(private val zipCode: Long,
2          private val forecastProvider: ForecastProvider = ForecastProvider()) :
3          Command<ForecastList> {
4
5      companion object {
6          const val DAYS = 7
7      }
8
9      override fun execute(): ForecastList =
10          forecastProvider.requestByZipCode(zipCode, DAYS)
11 }
```

The rest of code modifications consist of some renames and changes in package structure here and there. Take a look at the corresponding branch at Kotlin for Android Developers repository[46].

---

[46]https://github.com/antoniolg/Kotlin-for-Android-Developers/tree/chapter-21

22. Flow control and ranges

I have been using some conditional expressions in our code, so you are not new to some of the concepts of this chapter. But now it is time to explain them in more depth. Though in Kotlin we usually need fewer mechanisms to control the flow of the code that we would typically use in an entirely procedural programming language (some of them even practically disappear), they are still useful. There are also new powerful ideas that solve some particular problems much easier.

22.1 If Expression

Almost everything in Kotlin is an expression, which means it returns a value. If conditions are not an exception, so though we can use if as we are used to doing:

```
1   if (x > 0) {
2       toast("x is greater than 0")
3   } else if (x == 0) {
4       toast("x equals 0")
5   } else {
6       toast("x is smaller than 0")
7   }
```

We can also assign its result to a variable. We have used it like that several times in our code:

```
1   val res = if (x != null && x.size() >= days) x else null
```

This also implies that we do not need a ternary operation similar to the Java one because we can solve it easily with:

```
1  val z = if (condition) x else y
```

So the if expression always returns a value. If one of the branches returns Unit, the whole expression returns Unit, which can be ignored, and it will behave like a regular Java if condition in that case.

22.2 When expression

When expressions are similar to switch/case in Java, but far more powerful. This expression tries to match its argument against all possible branches sequentially until it finds one that is satisfied. It then applies the right side of the expression. The difference with a switch/case in Java is that the argument can be literally anything, and the conditions for the branches too.

For the default option, we can add an else branch that will be executed if none of the previous conditions are satisfied. The code executed when a condition is satisfied can be a block too:

```
1  when (x) {
2      1 -> println("x == 1")
3      2 -> println("x == 2")
4      else -> {
5          println("I'm a block")
6          println("x is neither 1 nor 2")
7      }
8  }
```

As it is an expression, it can return a result too. Take into consideration that when it is used as an expression, it must cover all the possible cases or implement the else branch. It will not compile otherwise:

```
1  val result = when (x) {
2      0, 1 -> "binary"
3      else -> "error"
4  }
```

As you can see, the condition can be a set of values separated by commas. However, it can be many more things. We could, for instance, check the type of the argument and make decisions based on this:

```
1  when(view) {
2      is TextView -> view.text = "I'm a TextView"
3      is EditText -> toast("EditText value: ${view.getText()}")
4      is ViewGroup -> toast("Number of children: ${view.getChildCount()} ")
5      else -> view.visibility = View.GONE
6  }
```

The argument is automatically converted in the right part of the condition, so you do not need to do any explicit casting.

It is possible to check whether the argument is inside a range (I will explain ranges later in this chapter), or even inside a collection:

```
1  val cost = when(x) {
2      in 1..10 -> "cheap"
3      in 10..100 -> "regular"
4      in 100..1000 -> "expensive"
5      in specialValues -> "special value!"
6      else -> "not rated"
7  }
```

Alternatively, you could also get rid of the argument and do any crazy checks you may need. It could easily substitute an if / else chain:

```
1  val res = when {
2      x in 1..10 -> "cheap"
3      s.contains("hello") -> "it's a welcome!"
4      v is ViewGroup -> "child count: ${v.getChildCount()}"
5      else -> ""
6  }
```

22.3 For loops

Though you will not use them too much if you make use of functional operators in collections, for loops can be useful in some situations, so they are still available. It works with anything that provides an iterator:

```
1  for (item in collection) {
2      print(item)
3  }
```

If we want to achieve the regular iteration over indices, we can also do it using ranges:

```
1  for (index in 0..viewGroup.getChildCount() - 1) {
2      val view = viewGroup.getChildAt(index)
3      view.visibility = View.VISIBLE
4  }
```

When iterating over an array or a list, we can make uses of existing properties that return a set of indices, so the previous artifact is not necessary:

```
1  for (i in array.indices)
2      print(array[i])
```

22.4 While and do/while loops

You can keep using while loops too, though they are not very common in Kotlin either. There are usually simpler and more visual ways to resolve this problem. A couple of examples:

```
1  while (x > 0) {
2      x--
3  }
4
5  do {
6      val y = retrieveData()
7  } while (y != null) // y is visible here!
```

22.5 Ranges

It is challenging to explain flow control without talking about ranges. But their scope is broader. Range expressions make use of an operator in the form of "..." that is defined implementing a rangeTo function.

Ranges help simplify our code in many creative ways. For instance we can convert this:

```
1   if (i >= 0 && i <= 10)
2       println(i)
```

Into this:

```
1   if (i in 0..10)
2       println(i)
```

Kotlin defines ranges for any types that can be compared, but for numerical types the compiler optimizes it by converting it to simpler analog code in Java, to avoid the extra overhead. The numerical ranges are also iterable, and the loops are optimized too by converting them to the same bytecode a for with indices would use in Java:

```
1   for (i in 0..10)
2       println(i)
```

Ranges are incremental by default, so something like:

```
1   for (i in 10..0)
2       println(i)
```

Would do nothing. You can, however, use the function downTo:

```
1   for (i in 10 downTo 0)
2       println(i)
```

We can define a spacing different from 1 among the values in a range by using step:

```
1   for (i in 1..4 step 2) println(i)
2
3   for (i in 4 downTo 1 step 2) println(i)
```

If you want to create an open range (which excludes the last item), you can use the function until:

```
1    for (i in 0 until 4) println(i)
```

This previous line prints from 0 to 3, but skips the last value. This means that `0 until 4 == 0..3`. For iterations over lists, it could be easier to understand if we use `for (i in 0 until list.size)` instead of `for (i in 0..list.size - 1)`.

As mentioned before, there are really creative ways to use ranges. For instance, an easy way to get the list of `Views` inside a `ViewGroup` would be:

```
1    val views = (0 until viewGroup.childCount).map { viewGroup.getChildAt(it) }
```

The mix of ranges and functional operators prevents from having to use an explicit loop to iterate over the collection and the creation of an explicit list where we add the views. You can do everything on a single line.

If you want to know more about how to implement ranges and see more examples and useful information, you can go to Kotlin reference[47].

---

[47]https://kotlinlang.org/docs/reference/ranges.html

23 Creating a Detail Activity

When we click on an item from the home screen, we would expect to navigate to a detail activity and see some extra info about the forecast for that day. We are currently showing a toast after an item click, but it is time to change that.

23.1 Preparing the request

As we need to know which item we are going to show in the detail activity, logic tells we need to send the *id* of the forecast to the detail. So the domain model needs a new *id* property:

domain/model/DomainClasses.kt

```
data class Forecast(val id: Long, val date: Long, val description: String,
    val high: Int, val low: Int, val iconUrl: String)
```

The ForecastProvider also needs a new function, which returns the requested forecast by id. The DetailActivity will use it to recover the forecast based on the id it will receive. As all the requests always iterate over the sources and return the first non-null result, we can extract that behaviour to another function:

domain/datasource/ForecastProvider.kt

```
private fun <T : Any> requestToSources(f: (ForecastDataSource) -> T?): T
        = sources.firstResult { f(it) }
```

The function is generified using a non-nullable type. It will receive a function which uses a ForecastDataSource to return a nullable object of the generic type, and will finally return a non-nullable object. We can rewrite the previous request and write the new one this way:

domain/datasource/ForecastProvider.kt

```
1  fun requestByZipCode(zipCode: Long, days: Int): ForecastList = requestToSources {
2      val res = it.requestForecastByZipCode(zipCode, todayTimeSpan())
3      if (res != null && res.size() >= days) res else null
4  }
5
6  fun requestForecast(id: Long): Forecast = requestToSources {
7      it.requestDayForecast(id)
8  }
```

Now the data sources need to implement the new function:

domain/datasource/ForecastDataSource.kt

```
1  fun requestDayForecast(id: Long): Forecast?
```

The `ForecastDb` will always have the required value already cached from previous requests, so we can get it from there this way:

data/db/ForecastDb.kt

```
1  override fun requestDayForecast(id: Long): Forecast? = forecastDbHelper.use {
2      val forecast = select(DayForecastTable.NAME).byId(id).
3              parseOpt { DayForecast(HashMap(it)) }
4
5      if (forecast != null) dataMapper.convertDayToDomain(forecast) else null
6  }
```

The `select` query is very similar to the previous one. I created another utility function called `byId`, because a request by *id* is so common that a function like that simplifies the process and is easier to read. The implementation of the function is quite simple:

extensions/DatabaseExtensions.kt

```
1  fun SelectQueryBuilder.byId(id: Long)
2          = whereSimple("_id = ?", id.toString())
```

It makes use of the `whereSimple` function and implements the search over the `_id` field. This function is quite generic, but as you can see, you could create as many extension functions as you need based on the structure of your database, and hugely simplify the readability of your code. The DbDataMapper has some slight changes not worth mentioning. You can check them in the repository.

On the other hand, the ForecastServer is never used, because the info is always cached in the database. We could implement it to defend our code from uncommon edge cases, but we are not doing it in this case, so it will just throw an exception if the function is called:

data/server/ForecastServer.kt

```
1   override fun requestDayForecast(id: Long)
2           = throw UnsupportedOperationException()
```

try **and** throw **are expressions**

In Kotlin, almost everything is an expression, which means it returns a value. This is really important for functional programming, and particularly useful when dealing with edge cases with try-catch or when throwing exceptions. For instance, the example above shows how we can assign an exception to the result even if they are not of the same type, instead of having to create a full block of code. This is very useful too when we want to throw an exception in one of when branches:

```
1   val x = when(y) {
2       in 0..10 -> 1
3       in 11..20 -> 2
4       else -> throw Exception("Invalid")
5   }
```

The same happens with try-catch, we can assign a value depending on the result of the try:

```
1   val x = try { doSomething() } catch { null }
```

The last thing we need to be able to perform the request from the new activity is to create a command. The code is really simple:

domain/commands/RequestDayForecastCommand.kt

```
1  class RequestDayForecastCommand(
2          val id: Long,
3          private val forecastProvider: ForecastProvider = ForecastProvider()) :
4          Command<Forecast> {
5
6      override fun execute() = forecastProvider.requestForecast(id)
7  }
```

The request returns a `Forecast` result that is used by the activity to draw its UI.

23.2 Providing a new activity

We are now prepared to create the `DetailActivity`.

In Android Studio 2.3 and below, you can select the package where you want to create the activity, right click and select `New -> Kotlin Activity`.

For Android Studio 3.0, the wizard already allows selecting the language. Choose `New -> Activity` and the type of activity you want to create. There is a `Source Language` drop-down at the end of the screen that you can use to change the language to Kotlin.

Our detail activity receives a couple of parameters from the main one: the forecast id and the name of the city. The first one is used to request the data from the database, and the name of the city fills the toolbar. So we first need a couple of names to identify the parameters in the bundle:

ui/activities/DetailActivity.kt

```
1  public class DetailActivity : AppCompatActivity() {
2
3      companion object {
4          const val ID = "DetailActivity:id"
5          const val CITY_NAME = "DetailActivity:cityName"
6      }
7      ...
8  }
```

In onCreate function, the first step is to set the content view. The UI will be really simple, but more than enough for this app example:

layout/activity_detail.xml

```
1   <LinearLayout
2       xmlns:android="http://schemas.android.com/apk/res/android"
3       xmlns:tools="http://schemas.android.com/tools"
4       android:layout_width="match_parent"
5       android:layout_height="match_parent"
6       android:orientation="vertical"
7       android:paddingBottom="@dimen/activity_vertical_margin"
8       android:paddingLeft="@dimen/activity_horizontal_margin"
9       android:paddingRight="@dimen/activity_horizontal_margin"
10      android:paddingTop="@dimen/activity_vertical_margin">
11
12      <LinearLayout
13          android:layout_width="match_parent"
14          android:layout_height="wrap_content"
15          android:orientation="horizontal"
16          android:gravity="center_vertical"
17          tools:ignore="UseCompoundDrawables">
18
19          <ImageView
20              android:id="@+id/icon"
21              android:layout_width="64dp"
22              android:layout_height="64dp"
23              tools:src="@mipmap/ic_launcher"
24              tools:ignore="ContentDescription"/>
25
26          <TextView
27              android:id="@+id/weatherDescription"
28              android:layout_width="wrap_content"
29              android:layout_height="wrap_content"
30              android:layout_margin="@dimen/spacing_xlarge"
31              android:textAppearance="@style/TextAppearance.AppCompat.Display1"
32              tools:text="Few clouds"/>
33
34      </LinearLayout>
35
36      <LinearLayout
37          android:layout_width="match_parent"
38          android:layout_height="wrap_content">
39
40          <TextView
41              android:id="@+id/maxTemperature"
42              android:layout_width="0dp"
43              android:layout_height="wrap_content"
```

```
44              android:layout_weight="1"
45              android:layout_margin="@dimen/spacing_xlarge"
46              android:gravity="center_horizontal"
47              android:textAppearance="@style/TextAppearance.AppCompat.Display3"
48              tools:text="30"/>
49
50          <TextView
51              android:id="@+id/minTemperature"
52              android:layout_width="0dp"
53              android:layout_height="wrap_content"
54              android:layout_weight="1"
55              android:layout_margin="@dimen/spacing_xlarge"
56              android:gravity="center_horizontal"
57              android:textAppearance="@style/TextAppearance.AppCompat.Display3"
58              tools:text="10"/>
59
60      </LinearLayout>
61
62  </LinearLayout>
```

Then assign it from onCreate code. Use the city name to fill the toolbar title. The methods for intent and title are automatically mapped to a property:

ui/activities/DetailActivity.kt

```
1  setContentView(R.layout.activity_detail)
2  title = intent.getStringExtra(CITY_NAME)
```

The other part in onCreate implements the call to the command. It is very similar to the call we previously did:

ui/activities/DetailActivity.kt

```
1  doAsync {
2      val result = RequestDayForecastCommand(intent.getLongExtra(ID, -1)).execute()
3      uiThread { bindForecast(result) }
4  }
```

When the result is recovered from the database, the bindForecast function is called in the UI thread. I am using Kotlin Android Extensions plugin again in this activity, to get the properties from the XML without using findViewById:

ui/activities/DetailActivity.kt

```
1   import kotlinx.android.synthetic.main.activity_detail.*
2
3   ...
4
5   private fun bindForecast(forecast: Forecast) = with(forecast) {
6       Picasso.with(this@DetailActivity).load(iconUrl).into(icon)
7       supportActionBar?.subtitle = date.toDateString(DateFormat.FULL)
8       weatherDescription.text = description
9       bindWeather(high to maxTemperature, low to minTemperature)
10  }
```

There are some interesting things here. For instance, I am creating another extension function able to convert a Long object into a visual date string. Remember we were using it in the adapter too, so it is a good moment to extract it into a function:

extensions/ExtensionUtils.kt

```
1   fun Long.toDateString(dateFormat: Int = DateFormat.MEDIUM): String {
2       val df = DateFormat.getDateInstance(dateFormat, Locale.getDefault())
3       return df.format(this)
4   }
```

It gets a date format (or use the default DateFormat.MEDIUM) and converts the Long into a String that is understandable by the user.

Another interesting function is bindWeather. It gets a vararg of pairs of Int and TextView, and assigns a text and a text color to the TextViews based on the temperature.

ui/activities/DetailActivity.kt

```
1   private fun bindWeather(vararg views: Pair<Int, TextView>) = views.forEach {
2       it.second.text = "${it.first}"
3       it.second.textColor = color(when (it.first) {
4           in -50..0 -> android.R.color.holo_red_dark
5           in 0..15 -> android.R.color.holo_orange_dark
6           else -> android.R.color.holo_green_dark
7       })
8   }
```

For each pair, it assigns the text that shows the temperature and a color based on the value of the temperature: red for low temperatures, orange for mild ones and green for the rest. The values are random, but it is a good illustration of what we can do with a when expression, how clean and short the code becomes.

color is an extension function I miss from Anko, which simplifies the way to get a color from resources, similar to the dimen one we have used in some other places. At the time of writing this lines, current support library relies on the class ContextCompat to get a color in a compatible way for all Android versions:

extensions/ContextExtensions.kt

```
1   public fun Context.color(res: Int): Int = ContextCompat.getColor(this, res)
```

I was missing a property representation for textColor. The thing is TextView lacks getTextColor() method, so it is not automatically parsed. A definition could be this one:

extensions/ViewExtensions.kt

```
1   var TextView.textColor: Int
2       get() = currentTextColor
3       set(v) = setTextColor(v)
```

There is an implementation in another Anko package (it returns an exception in get, it could be an alternative), the one related to the creation of views using a DSL. If you are implementing your views using regular XML, I recommend not to add this library if you are using one or two functions. That library is big, and you will waste a good part of method count.

The AndroidManifest also needs to be aware that a new activity exists:

AndroidManifest.xml

```
1  <activity
2      android:name=".ui.activities.DetailActivity"
3      android:parentActivityName=".ui.activities.MainActivity" >
4      <meta-data
5          android:name="android.support.PARENT_ACTIVITY"
6          android:value="com.antonioleiva.weatherapp.ui.activities.MainActivity" />
7  </activity>
```

23.3 Start an activity: reified functions

The final step consists of starting the detail activity from the main activity. We can rewrite the adapter instantiation this way:

```
1  val adapter = ForecastListAdapter(result) {
2      val intent = Intent(MainActivity@this, javaClass<DetailActivity>())
3      intent.putExtra(DetailActivity.ID, it.id)
4      intent.putExtra(DetailActivity.CITY_NAME, result.city)
5      startActivity(intent)
6  }
```

But this is too verbose. As usual, Anko provides a much simpler way to start an activity by using a **reified function**:

ui/activities/MainActivity.kt

```
1  val adapter = ForecastListAdapter(result) {
2      startActivity<DetailActivity>(DetailActivity.ID to it.id,
3              DetailActivity.CITY_NAME to result.city)
4  }
```

What is the magic behind reified functions? As you may know, when we create a generic method in Java, there is no way to get the class from the generic type. A popular workaround is to pass the class as a parameter. In Kotlin, an inline function can be reified, which means we can get and use the class of the generic type inside the function. In this case, we can create the intent inside the function, by calling `T::class.javaClass`. A simpler version of what Anko does would be the next (I am only using `String` extras in this example):

```
1  public inline fun <reified T: Activity> Context.startActivity(
2          vararg params: Pair<String, String>) {
3
4      val intent = Intent(this, T::class.java)
5      params.forEach { intent.putExtra(it.first, it.second) }
6      startActivity(intent)
7  }
```

The real implementation is a bit more complicated because it uses a long and a boring when expression to add the extras depending on the type, but it does not add much useful knowledge to the concept.

Reified functions are, once more, a syntactic sugar that simplifies the code and improves its comprehension. In this case, it creates an intent by getting the javaClass from the generic type, iterates over params and adds them to the intent, and starts the activity using the intent. The reified type is limited to be an Activity descendant.

The rest of little details are covered in the repository[48]. We now have a simple (but complete) master-detail App implemented in Kotlin without using a single line of Java.

---

[48]https://github.com/antoniolg/Kotlin-for-Android-Developers/tree/chapter-23

24 Interfaces and Delegation

24.1 Interfaces

Interfaces in Kotlin are more powerful than in Java 7. If you have worked with Java 8, similarities are much closer there. In Kotlin, we can use interfaces the same way as in Java. Imagine we have some animals, and some of them can fly. This is the interface we could have for flying animals:

```
1   interface FlyingAnimal {
2       fun fly()
3   }
```

Both birds and bats can fly by moving their wings. So let's create a couple of classes for them:

```
1   class Bird : FlyingAnimal {
2       val wings: Wings = Wings()
3       override fun fly() = wings.move()
4   }
5
6   class Bat : FlyingAnimal {
7       val wings: Wings = Wings()
8       override fun fly() = wings.move()
9   }
```

When a couple of classes extend from an interface, it is very typical they both share the same implementation. However, Java 7 interfaces can only define the behavior, but not implement it.

Kotlin interfaces, on the other hand, can implement functions. The only difference from a class is that they are stateless, so the properties that need a backing field need to be overridden by the class. The class is in charge of saving the state of interface properties.

We can make the interface implement the fly function:

```
1  interface FlyingAnimal {
2      val wings: Wings
3      fun fly() = wings.move()
4  }
```

As mentioned, classes need to override the property:

```
1  class Bird : FlyingAnimal {
2      override val wings: Wings = Wings()
3  }
4
5  class Bat : FlyingAnimal {
6      override val wings: Wings = Wings()
7  }
```

And now both birds and bats can fly:

```
1  val bird = Bird()
2  val bat = Bat()
3
4  bird.fly()
5  bat.fly()
```

24.2 Delegation

The delegation[49] is a handy pattern that can be used to extract responsibilities from a class. The delegation pattern is supported natively by Kotlin, so it prevents the need of calling the delegate. The delegator just needs to specify which instance implements the interface.

In our previous example, we can specify how the animal flies through the constructor, instead of implementing it. For instance, a flying animal that uses wings to fly can be implemented this way:

---

[49]https://en.wikipedia.org/wiki/Delegation_pattern

```
1  interface CanFly {
2      fun fly()
3  }
4
5  class Bird(f: CanFly) : CanFly by f
```

We can indicate that a bird can fly by using the interface, but the way the bird uses to fly is defined by a delegate that comes through the constructor, so we can have different birds with different flying methods. The way an animal with wings flies is defined in another class:

```
1  class AnimalWithWings : CanFly {
2      val wings: Wings = Wings()
3      override fun fly() = wings.move()
4  }
```

An animal with wings moves its wings to be able to fly. So now we can create a bird that flies using wings:

```
1  val birdWithWings = Bird(AnimalWithWings())
2  birdWithWings.fly()
```

But now wings can be used with other animals that are not birds. If we assume that bats always use wings, we could instantiate the object directly where we specify the delegation:

```
1  class Bat : CanFly by AnimalWithWings()
2  ...
3  val bat = Bat()
4  bat.fly()
```

24.3 Implementing an example in our App

Interfaces can be used to extract common code from classes which have some similar behavior. For instance, we can create an interface that deals with the toolbar of the app. Both `MainActivity` and `DetailActivity` share similar code that deals with the toolbar.

But first, some changes need to be done to start using a toolbar included in the layout instead of the standard `ActionBar`. The first thing will be extending a `NoActionBar` theme. That way, the toolbar is not included automatically:

values/styles.xml

```
1   <style name="AppTheme" parent="Theme.AppCompat.Light.NoActionBar">
2       <item name="colorPrimary">#ff212121</item>
3       <item name="colorPrimaryDark">@android:color/black</item>
4   </style>
```

We are using a light theme. Next, let's create a toolbar layout that we can include later in some other layouts:

layout/toolbar.xml

```
1   <android.support.v7.widget.Toolbar
2       xmlns:app="http://schemas.android.com/apk/res-auto"
3       xmlns:android="http://schemas.android.com/apk/res/android"
4       android:id="@+id/toolbar"
5       android:layout_width="match_parent"
6       android:layout_height="?attr/actionBarSize"
7       android:background="?attr/colorPrimary"
8       android:theme="@style/ThemeOverlay.AppCompat.Dark.ActionBar"
9       app:popupTheme="@style/ThemeOverlay.AppCompat.Light"/>
```

The toolbar specifies its background, a dark theme for itself and a light theme for the popups it generates (the overflow menu for instance). We get then the same theme we already had: a light theme with dark Action Bar.

Next step will be modifying the `MainActivity` layout to include the toolbar:

layout/activity_main.xml

```
1   <FrameLayout
2       xmlns:android="http://schemas.android.com/apk/res/android"
3       android:layout_width="match_parent"
4       android:layout_height="match_parent">
5
6       <android.support.v7.widget.RecyclerView
7           android:id="@+id/forecastList"
8           android:layout_width="match_parent"
9           android:layout_height="match_parent"
10          android:clipToPadding="false"
11          android:paddingTop="?attr/actionBarSize"/>
12
13      <include layout="@layout/toolbar"/>
14
15  </FrameLayout>
```

Now that we have added the toolbar to the layout, we can start using it. We are creating an interface that will let us:

- Change the title
- Specify whether it shows the up navigation action or not
- Animate the toolbar when scrolling
- Assign the same menu to all activities and an event for the actions

So let's define the `ToolbarManager`:

ui/activities/ToolbarManager.kt

```
1   interface ToolbarManager {
2       val toolbar: Toolbar
3       ...
4   }
```

It needs a toolbar property. Interfaces are stateless, so the property can be defined, but no value can be assigned. Classes that implement it require overriding the property.

On the other hand, we can implement stateless properties without the need of being overridden. That is, properties that can work without using a backing field. An example would be a property which deals with the toolbar title:

ui/activities/ToolbarManager.kt

```
1   var toolbarTitle: String
2       get() = toolbar.title.toString()
3       set(value) {
4           toolbar.title = value
5       }
```

As the property just uses the toolbar, it does not need to save additional state.

We are now creating a new function that initializes the toolbar, by inflating a menu and setting a listener:

ui/activities/ToolbarManager.kt

```
1   fun initToolbar() {
2       toolbar.inflateMenu(R.menu.menu_main)
3       toolbar.setOnMenuItemClickListener {
4           when (it.itemId) {
5               R.id.action_settings -> App.instance.toast("Settings")
6               else -> App.instance.toast("Unknown option")
7           }
8           true
9       }
10  }
```

We can also add a function that enables the navigation icon in the toolbar, sets an arrow icon and a listener that will be fired when the icon is pressed:

ui/activities/ToolbarManager.kt

```
1   fun enableHomeAsUp(up: () -> Unit) {
2       toolbar.navigationIcon = createUpDrawable()
3       toolbar.setNavigationOnClickListener { up() }
4   }
5
6   private fun createUpDrawable() =
7           DrawerArrowDrawable(toolbar.ctx).apply { progress = 1f }
```

The function receives the listener, creates the up drawable by using the DrawerArrowDrawable[50] on its final state (when the arrow is already showing) and assigns the listener to the toolbar.

---

[50]https://developer.android.com/reference/android/support/v7/graphics/drawable/DrawerArrowDrawable.html

Finally, the interface provides a function that allows the toolbar to be attached to a scroll, and animates the toolbar depending on the direction of the scroll. The toolbar will be hidden while we are scrolling down and displayed again when scrolling up:

ui/activities/ToolbarManager.kt

```kotlin
fun attachToScroll(recyclerView: RecyclerView) {
    recyclerView.addOnScrollListener(object : RecyclerView.OnScrollListener() {
        override fun onScrolled(recyclerView: RecyclerView?, dx: Int, dy: Int) {
            if (dy > 0) toolbar.slideExit() else toolbar.slideEnter()
        }
    })
}
```

Let's create a couple of extension functions that animate the views in and out of the screen. They check if the animation has not been previously performed. That way it prevents the view from being animated every time the scroll varies:

extensions/ViewExtensions.kt

```kotlin
fun View.slideExit() {
    if (translationY == 0f) animate().translationY(-height.toFloat())
}

fun View.slideEnter() {
    if (translationY < 0f) animate().translationY(0f)
}
```

After implementing the toolbar manager, it is time to use it in the `MainActivity`, which now must implement the interface:

ui/activities/MainActivity.kt

```kotlin
class MainActivity : AppCompatActivity(), ToolbarManager {
    ...
}
```

We first specify the toolbar property. We can implement a lazy find so that the toolbar will be already inflated by the time we use it:

ui/activities/MainActivity.kt

```
1   override val toolbar by lazy { find<Toolbar>(R.id.toolbar) }
```

MainActivity will initialize the toolbar, attach to the RecyclerView scroll and modify the toolbar title:

ui/activities/MainActivity.kt

```
1   override fun onCreate(savedInstanceState: Bundle?) {
2       super.onCreate(savedInstanceState)
3       setContentView(R.layout.activity_main)
4       initToolbar()
5
6       forecastList.layoutManager = LinearLayoutManager(this)
7       attachToScroll(forecastList)
8
9       doAsync {
10          val result = RequestForecastCommand(94043).execute()
11          uiThread {
12              val adapter = ForecastListAdapter(result) {
13                  startActivity<DetailActivity>(DetailActivity.ID to it.id,
14                      DetailActivity.CITY_NAME to result.city)
15              }
16              forecastList.adapter = adapter
17              toolbarTitle = "${result.city} (${result.country})"
18          }
19      }
20  }
```

DetailActivity also needs some layout modifications:

layout/activity_detail.xml

```xml
1  <LinearLayout
2      xmlns:android="http://schemas.android.com/apk/res/android"
3      xmlns:tools="http://schemas.android.com/tools"
4      android:layout_width="match_parent"
5      android:layout_height="match_parent"
6      android:orientation="vertical">
7
8      <include layout="@layout/toolbar"/>
9
10     <LinearLayout
11         android:layout_width="match_parent"
12         android:layout_height="wrap_content"
13         android:orientation="horizontal"
14         android:gravity="center_vertical"
15         android:paddingTop="@dimen/activity_vertical_margin"
16         android:paddingLeft="@dimen/activity_horizontal_margin"
17         android:paddingRight="@dimen/activity_horizontal_margin"
18         tools:ignore="UseCompoundDrawables">
19         ....
20     </LinearLayout>
21
22 </LinearLayout>
```

The `toolbar` property is specified the same way. `DetailActivity` will initialize the toolbar too, set the title and enable the up navigation icon:

ui/activities/DetailActivity.kt

```kotlin
1  override fun onCreate(savedInstanceState: Bundle?) {
2      super.onCreate(savedInstanceState);
3      setContentView(R.layout.activity_detail)
4
5      initToolbar()
6      toolbarTitle = intent.getStringExtra(CITY_NAME)
7      enableHomeAsUp { onBackPressed() }
8      ...
9  }
```

Interfaces can help us extract common code from classes that share similar behaviors. It can be used as an alternative to composition, which keeps our code better organized and easier to reuse.

Think where interfaces can help you write better code, and check the new one in the branch of this chapter[51].

---

[51]https://github.com/antoniolg/Kotlin-for-Android-Developers/tree/chapter-24

25 Generics

Generic programming consists of writing algorithms without the need of specifying the exact type the code is going to use. That way, we can create functions or types that only differ in the set of types they use, improving code reusability. These units of code are known as generics, and they exist in many languages, including Java and Kotlin.

In Kotlin, generics are even more important, because the high presence of regular and extension functions increments the number of times that generics are of some use for us. Though we have been using them blindly throughout the book, generics are usually one of the trickiest parts of any language, so I am trying to explain it in the simplest possible way so that main ideas are clear enough.

25.1 Basics

For instance, we can create a class which specifies a generic type:

```
1    class TypedClass<T>(parameter: T) {
2        val value: T = parameter
3    }
```

This class now can be instantiated using any type, and the parameter will use the type in the definition. We could do:

```
1    val t1 = TypedClass<String>("Hello World!")
2    val t2 = TypedClass<Int>(25)
```

But Kotlin is all about simplicity and boilerplate reduction, so if the compiler can infer the type of the parameter, we do not even need to specify it:

```
1   val t1 = TypedClass("Hello World!")
2   val t2 = TypedClass(25)
3   val t3 = TypedClass<String?>(null)
```

As the third object is receiving a null reference, the type still needs to be specified because the compiler cannot infer it.

We can go beyond and, as in Java, reduce the types that can be used in a generic class by setting it in the definition. For instance, if we want to restrict the previous class to non-nullable types, we do:

```
1   class TypedClass<T : Any>(parameter: T) {
2       val value: T = parameter
3   }
```

If you compile previous code, you will see that t3 now throws an error. Nullable types are not allowed anymore. But restrictions can be obviously more strict. What if we want to accept only classes that extend Context? Easy:

```
1   class TypedClass<T : Context>(parameter: T) {
2       val value: T = parameter
3   }
4
5   val t1 = TypedClass(activity)
6   val t2 = TypedClass(context)
7   val t3 = TypedClass(service)
```

Now every class which extends Context can be used as the type of our class. The rest of types are not allowed.

Of course, types are also allowed in functions. We can build generic functions quite easily:

```
1   fun <T> typedFunction(item: T): List<T> {
2       ...
3   }
```

25.2 Variance

This is really one of the trickiest parts to understand. In Java, there is a problem when we use generic types. Logic says that List<String> should be able to be casted to List<Object> because it is less restrictive. But take a look at this example:

```
1   List<String> strList = new ArrayList<>();
2   List<Object> objList = strList;
3   objList.add(5);
4   String str = objList.get(0);
```

If the Java compiler allowed us to do this, we could add an Integer to an Object list, and this would crash at some point. That is why wildcards were added to the language. Wildcards increase flexibility while limiting this problem.

If we add '? extends Object' we are using **covariance**, which means that we can deal with any object that uses a type that is more restrictive than Object, but we can only do get operations safely. If we want to copy a collection of Strings into a collection of Objects, we should be allowed, right?

Then, if we have:

```
1   List<String> strList = ...;
2   List<Object> objList = ...;
3   objList.addAll(strList);
```

This is possible because the definition of addAll() in Collection interface is something like:

```
1   List<String>
2   interface Collection<E> ... {
3     void addAll(Collection<? extends E> items);
4   }
```

Otherwise, without the wildcard, we would not be allowed to use a String list with this method. The opposite, of course, would fail. We cannot use addAll() to add a list of Objects to a list of Strings. As we are only getting the items from the collection we use in that method, it is a perfect example of covariance.

On the other hand, we can find **contravariance**, which is just the opposite situation. Following with the Collection example, if we want to add items to a Collection we are passing as a parameter, we could add objects with a more restrictive type into a more generic collection. For instance, we could add Strings to an Object list:

```
1   void copyStrings(Collection<? super String> to, Collection<String> from) {
2       to.addAll(from);
3   }
```

The only restriction we have to add Strings to another collection is that the collection accepts Objects that are Strings or parent classes.

But wildcards have some limitations. Wildcards define **use-site variance**, which means we need to declare them where we use them. This implies adding boilerplate every time we declare a more generic variable.

Let's see an example. Using a class similar to the one we had before:

```
1   public class TypedClass<T> {
2       public T doSomething(){
3           . . .
4       }
5   }
```

This code will not compile:

```
1   TypedClass<String> t1 = new TypedClass<>();
2   TypedClass<Object> t2 = t1;
```

Though it really does not make sense, because we could still keep calling all the methods of the class, and nothing would break. We need to specify that the type can have a more flexible definition.

```
1   TypedClass<String> t1 = new TypedClass<>();
2   TypedClass<? extends String> t2 = t1;
```

The use of wildcards, in this case, makes things more difficult to understand, and adds some extra boilerplate.

On the other hand, Kotlin deals with it more naturally by using **declaration-site variance**. In Kotlin, we specify that we can deal with less restrictive situations when defining the class or interface, and then we can use it blindly everywhere.

So let's see how it looks. Instead of long wildcards, Kotlin uses *out* for covariance and *in* for contravariance. In this case, as our class is producing objects that can be saved into less restrictive variables, we are using covariance. We can define this in the class declaration directly:

```
1   class TypedClass<out T>() {
2       fun doSomething(): T {
3           ...
4       }
5   }
```

And that is all we need. Now, the same example that would not compile in Java is perfectly possible in Kotlin:

```
1   val t1 = TypedClass<String>()
2   val t2: TypedClass<Any> = t1
```

If you were already used to these concepts, I am sure you can use *in* and *out* in Kotlin without any hassle. Otherwise, it requires a little practice and a good understanding of these concepts.

25.3 Generics examples

After the theory, let's move to some practical functions that will make our lives easier. Instead of reinventing the wheel, I am using three functions that are included in Kotlin standard library. These functions let us do remarkable things with just a generic implementation. They can inspire you to create your own functions.

let

let is a simple function that can be called by any object. It receives a function that takes the object as a parameter and returns the value that this function returns. It is handy to deal with nullable objects, for instance. Here it is the definition:

```
1    inline fun <T, R> T.let(f: (T) -> R): R = f(this)
```

It uses two generic types: T and R. The first type is defined by the calling object, and it is also the type that the lambda receives as the input argument. The second one is the result of the function.

How can we use it? You may remember that, when we were retrieving data from a data source, the result could be null. We then returned a result mapped to the domain model if it was not null, or just a null reference otherwise:

data/db/ForecastDb.kt

```
1    if (forecast != null) dataMapper.convertDayToDomain(forecast) else null
```

This can be improved. We should not need to deal with nullable types that way. We can avoid it by using let:

data/db/ForecastDb.kt

```
1    forecast?.let { dataMapper.convertDayToDomain(it) }
```

let function is only executed if forecast is not null thanks to '?.' operator. It returns null otherwise. Just what we were trying to achieve.

with

We have talked a lot about this function during the book. with receives an object and a lambda that behaves as an extension function. So we can use this inside the lambda to refer to the object. It also returns an object defined in the last line of the function.

```
1    inline fun <T, R> with(receiver: T, f: T.() -> R): R = receiver.f()
```

Generics work the same way here: T stands for the receiver type and R for the result. As you can see, the lambda is defined as an extension function by using this declaration: f: T.() -> R. That is why we can then call receiver.f().

We have several examples throughout the app:

data/db/DbDataMapper.kt

```
1  fun convertFromDomain(forecast: ForecastList) = with(forecast) {
2      val daily = dailyForecast.map { convertDayFromDomain(id, it) }
3      CityForecast(id, city, country, daily)
4  }
```

apply

It may look very similar to with function, but the idea is a bit different. apply can be used to avoid the creation of builders, because the object that calls the function can initialize itself the way it needs, and the apply function returns the same object:

```
1  inline fun <T> T.apply(f: T.() -> Unit): T { f(); return this }
```

We only need one generic type here, because the object that calls the function is also the returned value. A nice simple example would be:

```
1  val textView = TextView(context).apply {
2      text = "Hello"
3      hint = "Hint"
4      textColor = android.R.color.white
5  }
```

It creates a TextView, modifies some properties, and assigns it to a variable. Everything in a simple, readable and compact syntax. Let's use it in our current code. In ToolbarManager, we were doing this to create the navigation drawable:

```
1  private fun createUpDrawable() = with(DrawerArrowDrawable(toolbar.ctx)) {
2      progress = 1f
3      this
4  }
```

Using with and returning this is clearly something that can be done easier by using apply:

ui/activities/ToolbarManager.kt

```
1   private fun createUpDrawable() = DrawerArrowDrawable(toolbar.ctx).apply {
2       progress = 1f
3   }
```

You can review some more little improvements in Kotlin for Android Developers repository[52].

---

[52]https://github.com/antoniolg/Kotlin-for-Android-Developers/tree/chapter-25

26 Settings Screen

Until now, we have been using a default city to implement the app, but it is time add the ability to select another city. The app needs a settings section where the user can change the city.

We are going to stick to the zip code to identify the city. A real app would probably need more information because a zip code by itself does not identify a city in the whole world. But we at least will show a city around the world that uses the zip code we are defining in settings. This is a good chance to explain a different way to deal with preferences.

26.1 Creating the settings activity

A new activity will be opened when the settings option is selected in the overflow menu in the toolbar. So the first thing we need is a new SettingsActivity:

ui/activities/SettingsActivity.kt

```
1   class SettingsActivity : AppCompatActivity() {
2
3       override fun onCreate(savedInstanceState: Bundle?) {
4           super.onCreate(savedInstanceState)
5           setContentView(R.layout.activity_settings)
6           setSupportActionBar(toolbar)
7           supportActionBar?.setDisplayHomeAsUpEnabled(true)
8       }
9
10      override fun onOptionsItemSelected(item: MenuItem) = when (item.itemId) {
11          android.R.id.home -> {
12              onBackPressed()
13              true
14          }
15          else -> false
16      }
17  }
```

We will save the preference when the user gets out of the screen activity, so we are going to deal with the Up action the same way as the Back one, by redirecting the action to onBackPressed. Now, let's create the XML layout. A simple EditText is enough for the preference:

layout/activity_settings.xml

```
1   <FrameLayout
2       xmlns:android="http://schemas.android.com/apk/res/android"
3       android:layout_width="match_parent"
4       android:layout_height="match_parent">
5
6       <include layout="@layout/toolbar"/>
7
8       <LinearLayout
9           android:orientation="vertical"
10          android:layout_width="match_parent"
11          android:layout_height="match_parent"
12          android:layout_marginTop="?attr/actionBarSize"
13          android:padding="@dimen/spacing_xlarge">
14
15          <TextView
16              android:layout_width="wrap_content"
17              android:layout_height="wrap_content"
18              android:text="@string/city_zipcode"/>
19
20          <EditText
21              android:id="@+id/cityCode"
22              android:layout_width="match_parent"
23              android:layout_height="wrap_content"
24              android:hint="@string/city_zipcode"
25              android:inputType="number"/>
26
27      </LinearLayout>
28
29  </FrameLayout>
```

And then declare the activity in the AndroidManifest.xml:

AndroidManifest.xml

```
1  <activity
2      android:name=".ui.activities.SettingsActivity"
3      android:label="@string/settings"/>
```

26.2 Accessing Shared Preferences

You probably know what Android Shared Preferences[53] are. They consist of a set of keys and values that can be easily saved and restored by using the Android framework. These preferences are integrated with some parts of the SDK to make some tasks easier. Besides, since Android 6.0 (Marshmallow), shared preferences can be automatically cloud-saved, so when a user restores the app in a new device, these preferences are automatically recovered too.

Thanks to the use of property delegation, we can deal with preferences cleverly. We can create a delegate that queries the preference when get is called and saves it when we call to set.

As we want to save the zip code, which is a Long value, let's create a delegate for Long properties. In DelegatesExtensions.kt, implement a new LongPreference class:

extensions/DelegatesExtensions.kt

```
1  class LongPreference(
2          private val context: Context,
3          private val name: String, val default: Long) {
4
5      private val prefs by lazy {
6          context.getSharedPreferences("default", Context.MODE_PRIVATE)
7      }
8
9      operator fun getValue(thisRef: Any?, property: KProperty<*>): Long =
10         prefs.getLong(name, default)
11
12     operator fun setValue(thisRef: Any?, property: KProperty<*>, value: Long) {
13         prefs.edit().putLong(name, value).apply()
14     }
15 }
```

---

[53]http://developer.android.com/training/basics/data-storage/shared-preferences.html

First, we create a lazy access to preferences. That way, if we do not use the property, this delegate never requests the SharedPreferences object.

When get is called, its implementation uses the preferences instance to retrieve a long property with the name that was specified in the delegate declaration, and defaulting to the default value if the property is not found. When a value is set, it requests a preferences editor that saves the value using the name of the property.

We can then define the new delegate in the DelegatesExt object, so that it is easier to access when required:

extensions/DelegatesExtensions.kt

```
1   object DelegatesExt {
2       ....
3       fun longPreference(context: Context, name: String, default: Long) =
4           LongPreference(context, name, default)
5   }
```

In SettingsActivity, we can now define a property to deal with the zip code preference. I am also creating a couple of constants which keep the name and the default value of the property. That way they can be used in other sections of the App.

ui/activities/SettingsActivity.kt

```
1   companion object {
2       const val ZIP_CODE = "zipCode"
3       const val DEFAULT_ZIP = 94043L
4   }
5
6   private var zipCode: Long
7           by DelegatesExt.longPreference(this, ZIP_CODE, DEFAULT_ZIP)
```

Now it is easy to work with this preference. In onCreate, we get the value of the property and assign it to the EditText:

ui/activities/SettingsActivity.kt

```
1  override fun onCreate(savedInstanceState: Bundle?) {
2      ...
3      cityCode.setText(zipCode.toString())
4  }
```

We cannot use the self-generated property `text` because `EditText` returns an `Editable` in `getText`, so the property defaults to that value. If we try to assign a `String`, the compiler will complain. Using `setText()` will be enough.

Now we have everything we need to implement `onBackPressed`. Here, the new value of the property is saved:

ui/activities/SettingsActivity.kt

```
1  override fun onBackPressed() {
2      super.onBackPressed()
3      zipCode = cityCode.text.toString().toLong()
4  }
```

The `MainActivity` requires some little changes. First, it also needs a `zipCode` property.

ui/activities/MainActivity.kt

```
1  private val zipCode: Long by DelegatesExt.longPreference(this,
2          SettingsActivity.ZIP_CODE, SettingsActivity.DEFAULT_ZIP)
```

Moreover, I am moving the forecast load to `onResume` so that every time the activity is resumed, it refreshes the data, just in case the zip code changed. Of course, there are more efficient ways to do this, by checking whether the zip code changed before requesting the forecast again, for instance. But I want to keep this example simple, and the local database already keeps the requested info, so this solution is not that bad:

ui/activities/MainActivity.kt

```
1   override fun onResume() {
2       super.onResume()
3       loadForecast()
4   }
5
6   private fun loadForecast() = doAsync {
7       val result = RequestForecastCommand(zipCode).execute()
8       uiThread {
9           val adapter = ForecastListAdapter(result) {
10              startActivity<DetailActivity>(DetailActivity.ID to it.id,
11                  DetailActivity.CITY_NAME to result.city)
12          }
13          forecastList.adapter = adapter
14          toolbarTitle = "${result.city} (${result.country})"
15      }
16  }
```

The `RequestForecastCommand` is now using the `zipCode` property instead of the previously fixed value.

There is just one more thing we must do: start the settings activity when the user clicks on the overflow action. In `ToolbarManager`, the `initToolbar` function requires a small change:

ui/activities/ToolbarManager.kt

```
1   when (it.itemId) {
2       R.id.action_settings -> toolbar.ctx.startActivity<SettingsActivity>()
3       else -> App.instance.toast("Unknown option")
4   }
```

26.3 Generic preference delegate

Now that we are generics experts, why not extending `LongPreference` to be used with any type that Shared Preferences support? Let's create a new `Preference` delegate:

extensions/DelegatesExtensions.kt

```
1   class Preference<T>(private val context: Context, private val name: String,
2       private val default: T) {
3
4       private val prefs by lazy {
5           context.getSharedPreferences("default", Context.MODE_PRIVATE)
6       }
7
8       operator fun getValue(thisRef: Any?, property: KProperty<*>): T =
9           findPreference(name, default)
10
11      operator fun setValue(thisRef: Any?, property: KProperty<*>, value: T) {
12          putPreference(name, value)
13      }
14      ...
15  }
```

This preference is very similar to what we had before. We just substituted the Long references with a generic type T, and called to a couple of functions that do the hard work. These functions are very simple, though a bit repetitive. They check the type and use the specific method from preferences. For instance, the findPreference function looks like this:

extensions/DelegatesExtensions.kt

```
1   private fun findPreference(name: String, default: T): T = with(prefs) {
2       val res: Any = when (default) {
3           is Long -> getLong(name, default)
4           is String -> getString(name, default)
5           is Int -> getInt(name, default)
6           is Boolean -> getBoolean(name, default)
7           is Float -> getFloat(name, default)
8           else -> throw IllegalArgumentException(
9               "This type can't be saved into Preferences")
10      }
11
12      res as T
13  }
```

And basically the same for putPreference function, but using the preferences editor and saving the result of when at the end, by calling apply():

extensions/DelegatesExtensions.kt

```
1  private fun putPreference(name: String, value: T) = with(prefs.edit()) {
2      when (value) {
3          is Long -> putLong(name, value)
4          is String -> putString(name, value)
5          is Int -> putInt(name, value)
6          is Boolean -> putBoolean(name, value)
7          is Float -> putFloat(name, value)
8          else -> throw IllegalArgumentException("This type can be saved into Preferences")
9      }.apply()
10 }
```

Now update `DelegatesExt` object and you are done:

extensions/DelegatesExtensions.kt

```
1  object DelegatesExt {
2      ...
3      fun <T> preference(context: Context, name: String, default: T)
4          = Preference(context, name, default)
5  }
```

After this chapter, the user can now access the settings screen and modify the zip code. That way, when they return to the main screen, the forecast is automatically refreshed with the new information. Check the rest of small tweaks in the repository[54].

---

[54]https://github.com/antoniolg/Kotlin-for-Android-Developers/tree/chapter-26

27 Coroutines since Kotlin 1.3

Coroutines are one of the most exciting features in Kotlin. With them, you can simplify the work of asynchronous tasks in an impressive way, and make the code much more readable and easy to understand.

With coroutines, you can write asynchronous code, which was traditionally written using the Callback pattern, using synchronous style. The return value of a function will provide the result of the asynchronous call.

How's this magic happening? We'll see it in a minute. But first, let's understand why coroutines are necessary.

Coroutines have been with us since Kotlin 1.1 as an experimental feature. But Kotlin 1.3 released the final API, and now they are production ready.

27.1 Coroutines goal: The problem

Imagine that you have a login screen where the user enters a user name, a password, and clicks login.

Your app, under the hood, needs to do a server request to validate the login, and another call to recover a list of friends to show it on the screen.

The code in Kotlin could be something like this:

```
1    progress.visibility = View.VISIBLE
2
3    userService.doLoginAsync(username, password) { user ->
4
5        userService.requestCurrentFriendsAsync(user) { friends ->
6
7            val finalUser = user.copy(friends = friends)
8            toast("User ${finalUser.name} has ${finalUser.friends.size} friends")
9
10           progress.visibility = View.GONE
11       }
12
13   }
```

The steps would be:

1. It shows the progress
2. It sends a request to the server to validate the login
3. Then with the result, it does another request to recover the friends' list
4. Finally, it hides the progress again

But things can get worse. Imagine that the API is not the best (I am sure you have been there), and you have to get another set of friends: the suggested friends. Then you need to merge them into a unique list.

You have two options here:

1. Do the second friends request after the first one, which is the simplest way but also not very efficient. The second request does not need the result from the first one
2. Run both requests at the same time and find a way to synchronize the callback results. This is pretty complex.

In a real App, a lazy (and pragmatic) programmer would probably choose the first one:

```
1   progress.visibility = View.VISIBLE
2
3   userService.doLoginAsync(username, password) { user ->
4
5       userService.requestCurrentFriendsAsync(user) { currentFriends ->
6
7           userService.requestSuggestedFriendsAsync(user) { suggestedFriends ->
8               val finalUser = user.copy(friends = currentFriends + suggestedFriends)
9               toast("User ${finalUser.name} has ${finalUser.friends.size} friends")
10
11              progress.visibility = View.GONE
12          }
13
14      }
15
16  }
```

The code starts becoming difficult to understand, and we see the feared callback hell: the next call is done inside the previous callback, so the indentation keeps growing and growing.

Thanks to Kotlin lambdas, it doesn't look too bad. But who knows if, in the future, you will need to add another request that makes this even more unmanageable.

Besides, remember that we took the easy path, which is also not very time effective.

27.2 What are coroutines?

In order to understand the coroutines easily, let's say that coroutines are like threads, but better.

First, because coroutines let you write your asynchronous code sequentially, dramatically reducing the cognitive load.

And second, because they are much more efficient. Several coroutines can be run using the same thread. So while the number of threads that you can run in an App is pretty limited, you can run as many coroutines as you need. The limit is almost infinite.

Coroutines are based on the idea of suspending functions. These are functions that can stop the execution of a coroutine at any point and then get the control back to the coroutine once the result is ready and the function has finished doing its work.

So coroutines are basically a safe place where suspending functions will not (normally) block the current thread. And I say normally because it depends on how we define them. We will see all this later.

```
1   coroutine {
2       progress.visibility = View.VISIBLE
3
4       val user = suspended { userService.doLogin(username, password) }
5       val currentFriends = suspended { userService.requestCurrentFriends(user) }
6
7       val finalUser = user.copy(friends = currentFriends)
8       toast("User ${finalUser.name} has ${finalUser.friends.size} friends")
9
10      progress.visibility = View.GONE
11  }
```

So in the example above, we have a common structure for a coroutine. We will have a coroutine builder, and a set of suspending functions that will suspend the execution of the coroutine until they have the result.

Then, you can use the result in the following line. Pretty much like sequential code. These two artifacts are the key, but take into account that coroutine and suspended do not exist with those names, they are there just so that you can see the structure without having to understand more complex concepts. We will see all those in a minute.

Suspending functions

Suspending functions have the ability to block the execution of the coroutine while they are doing their work. Once they finish, the result of the operation is returned and can be used in the next line.

```
1   val user = suspended { userService.doLogin(username, password) }
2   val currentFriends = suspended { userService.requestCurrentFriends(user) }
```

Suspending functions can run on the same or a different thread. It depends on how everything is set up. Suspending functions can only run inside a coroutine or inside another suspending function.

To declare your own suspending function, you just need to use the suspend reserved word:

```
1   suspend fun suspendingFunction() : Int  {
2       // Long running task
3       return 0
4   }
```

Getting back to the original example, a question you may be asking is where all this code is executed. Let's focus on just one line:

```
1   coroutine {
2       progress.visibility = View.VISIBLE
3       ...
4   }
```

Where do you think that this line will be run? Are you sure that it will be the UI thread? If it's not, your App will crash, so it is an important question.

And the answer is that it depends: it depends on the coroutine context.

Coroutine context

The coroutine context is a set of rules and configurations that define how the coroutine will be executed. Under the hood, it's a kind of map, with a set of possible keys and values.

For now, it's just enough for you to know that one of the possible configurations is the dispatcher that is used to identify the thread where the coroutine will be executed.

This dispatcher can be provided in two ways:

- Explicitly: we manually set the dispatcher that will be used
- By the coroutine scope: let's forget about scopes for now, but this would be the second option

To do it explicitly, the coroutine builder receives a coroutine context as a first parameter. So there, we can specify the dispatcher that will be used. Dispatchers implement CoroutineContext, so it can be used there:

```
1   coroutine(Dispatchers.Main) {
2       progress.visibility = View.VISIBLE
3       ...
4   }
```

Now, the line that changes the visibility is executed in the UI thread. That one, and everything inside that coroutine. But what happens to the suspending functions?

```
1   coroutine {
2       ...
3       val user = suspended { userService.doLogin(username, password) }
4       val currentFriends = suspended { userService.requestCurrentFriends(user) }
5       ...
6   }
```

Are those requests also run on the main thread? If that's the case, they will block it, so we would have a problem. The answer, again, it's that it depends.

Suspending functions have different ways to define the dispatcher that will be used. A very helpful function that the coroutines library provides is withContext.

withContext

This is a function that allows to easily change the context that will be used to run a part of the code inside a coroutine. This is a suspending function, so it means that it'll suspend the coroutine until the code inside is executed, no matter the dispatcher that it's used.

With that, we can make our suspending functions use a different thread:

```
1   suspend fun suspendLogin(username: String, password: String) =
2           withContext(Dispatchers.Main) {
3               userService.doLogin(username, password)
4           }
```

The code above would still keep using the main thread, so it would block the UI, but that can be easily changed by specifying a different dispatcher:

```
1    suspend fun suspendLogin(username: String, password: String) =
2            withContext(Dispatchers.IO) {
3                userService.doLogin(username, password)
4            }
```

Now, by using the IO dispatcher, we use a background thread to do it. `withContext` is a suspending function itself, so we don't need to use it inside another suspending function. Instead, we can do:

```
1    val user = withContext(Dispatchers.IO) { userService.doLogin(username, password) }
2    val currentFriends = withContext(Dispatchers.IO) {
3            userService.requestCurrentFriends(user)
4    }
```

You may be wondering what dispatchers we have and when to use them. So let's clarify that now!

Dispatchers

As we saw, dispatchers are coroutine contexts that specify the thread or threads that can be used by the coroutine to run its code. There are dispatchers that just use one thread (like Main) and others that define a pool of threads that will be optimized to run all the coroutines they receive.

If you remember, at the beginning we told that 1 thread can run many coroutines, so the system won't create 1 thread per coroutine, but will try to reuse the ones that are already alive.

We have four main dispatchers:

- Default: It will be used when no dispatcher is defined, but we can set it explicitly too. This dispatcher is used to run tasks that make intensive use of the CPU, mainly App computations, algorithms, etc. It can use as many threads as CPU cores. As these are intensive tasks, it doesn't make sense to have more running at the same time, because the CPU will be busy
- IO: You will use this one to run input/output operations. In general, all tasks that will block the thread while waiting for an answer from another system: server

requests, access to database, files, sensorsâ€¦ As they don't use the CPU, you can have many running at the same time, so the size of this thread pool is 64. Android Apps are all about interaction with the device and network requests, so you probably will use this one most of the time.

- Unconfined: if you don't care much what thread is used, you can use this one. It's difficult to predict what thread will be used, so don't use it unless you're very sure of what you're doing
- Main: this is a special dispatcher that is included in UI related coroutine libraries. In particular, in the Android one, it will use the UI thread.

You have now the power to control the elements, use it wisely ðŸ™,

Coroutine Builders

Now that you're able to change the execution thread in a breeze, you need to learn how to run a new coroutine. To do that, you'll use the coroutine builders.

We have different builders depending on what we want to do, and you could technically write your own. But for most cases, the ones that the library provides are more than enough. Let's see them:

runBlocking

This builder blocks the current thread until all the tasks inside that coroutine are finished. That goes against what we want to achieve with coroutines. So what's the use then?

runBlocking is very helpful to test suspending tasks. In your tests, wrap the suspending task you want to test with a runBlocking call, and you will be able to assert the result and prevent that the test finishes before the background task ends.

```
1   fun testSuspendingFunction() = runBlocking {
2       val res = suspendingTask1()
3       assertEquals(0, res)
4   }
```

But that's it. You probably won't use runBlocking for much more than that.

launch

This is the main builder. You'll use it a lot because it's the simplest way to create coroutines. As opposed to runBlocking, it won't block the current thread (if we use the proper dispatchers, of course).

This builder always needs a scope. We'll see scopes in the next section, but for now, let's just use the GlobalScope:

```
1   GlobalScope.launch(Dispatchers.Main) {
2       ...
3   }
```

launch returns a Job, which is another class that implements CoroutineContext.

Jobs have a couple of interesting functions that can be very helpful. But it's important to know that a job can have a parent job. That parent job have some control over their children, and that's where these functions come into play:

job.join

With this function, you can block the coroutine associated with that job until all the child jobs are finished. All the suspending functions that are called inside that coroutine are tied to this job, so when the job can find out when all those child jobs finish and then continue the execution.

```
1    val job = GlobalScope.launch(Dispatchers.Main) {
2
3        doCoroutineTask()
4
5        val res1 = suspendingTask1()
6        val res2 = suspendingTask2()
7
8        process(res1, res2)
9
10   }
11
12   job.join()
```

job.join() is a suspending function itself, so it needs to be called inside another coroutine.

job.cancel

This function will cancel all its associated child jobs. So if, for instance, the suspend-ingTask1() is running when cancel() is called, this won't return the value to res1 and suspendingTask2() will never be executed:

```
1    val job = GlobalScope.launch(Dispatchers.Main) {
2
3        doCoroutineTask()
4
5        val res1 = suspendingTask1()
6        val res2 = suspendingTask2()
7
8        process(res1, res2)
9
10   }
11
12   job.cancel()
```

job.cancel() is a regular function, so it doesn't require a coroutine to be called.

async

We have this other builder that you will see now that it's going to fix the second important problem we had in the original example.

async allows running several background tasks in parallel. It's not a suspending function itself, so when we run async the background process starts, but it immediately continues running the next line. async always needs to be called inside another coroutine, and it returns a specialized job that is called Deferred.

This object has a new function called await(), which is the blocking one. We'll call await() only when we need the result. If the result is not ready yet, the coroutine is suspended at that point. If we had the result already, it'll just return it and continue. This way, you can run as many background tasks as you need.

So in the example below, the first request is required to do the other two. But both friend requests can be done in parallel. Using withContext we are wasting a precious time:

```
1   GlobalScope.launch(Dispatchers.Main) {
2
3       val user = withContext(Dispatchers.IO) { userService.doLogin(username, password) }
4       val currentFriends =
5           withContext(Dispatchers.IO) { userService.requestCurrentFriends(user) }
6       val suggestedFriends =
7           withContext(Dispatchers.IO) { userService.requestSuggestedFriends(user) }
8
9       val finalUser = user.copy(friends = currentFriends + suggestedFriends)
10  }
```

If we imagine that each request takes 2 seconds, this would be taking 6 seconds (aprox) to finish. If we substitute that with async:

```
1   GlobalScope.launch(Dispatchers.Main) {
2
3       val user = withContext(Dispatchers.IO) { userService.doLogin(username, password) }
4       val currentFriends = async(Dispatchers.IO) { userService.requestCurrentFriends(user) }
5       val suggestedFriends =
6           async(Dispatchers.IO) { userService.requestSuggestedFriends(user) }
7
8       val finalUser = user.copy(friends = currentFriends.await() + suggestedFriends.await())
9
10  }
```

The second and the third tasks run in parallel, so they would (ideally) run at the same time, and the time would be reduced to 4 seconds.

Besides, synchronizing both results is trivial. Just call await on both and let the coroutines framework do the rest.

Scopes

So far we have a pretty decent code doing quite complex operations in a very simple way. But we still have a problem.

Imagine that we want to show these friends list in a RecyclerView, but while we are running one of the background tasks, the user decides to close the activity. The activity will now be in isFinishing state, so any UI update will throw an exception.

How can we solve this situation? With scopes. Let's see the different scopes we have:

Global scope

It's a general scope that can be used for any coroutines that are meant to continue executing while the App is running. So they shouldn't be tied to any specific components that can be destroyed.

We've used it before, so should be easy now:

```
1  GlobalScope.launch(Dispatchers.Main) {
2      ...
3  }
```

When you use GlobalScope, always ask yourself twice whether this coroutine affects the whole App and not just a specific screen or component.

Implement CoroutineScope

Any classes can implement this interface and become a valid scope. The only thing you need to do is to override the coroutineContext property.

Here, there are at least two important things to configure: the dispatcher, and the job.

If you remember, a context can be a combination of other contexts. They just need to be of different type. So here, in general, you will define two things:

- The dispatcher, to identify the default dispatcher that the coroutines will use
- The job, so that you can cancel all pending coroutines at any moment

```
1   class MainActivity : AppCompatActivity(), CoroutineScope {
2
3       override val coroutineContext: CoroutineContext
4           get() = Dispatchers.Main + job
5
6       private lateinit var job: Job
7
8   }
```

The plus(+) operation is used to combine contexts. If two contexts of different type are concatenated, it will create a CombinedContext that will have both configurations.

On the other hand, if two of the same type are concatenated, it will use the second one. So for instance: Dispatchers.Main + Dispatchers.IO == Dispatchers.IO

We create the job as lateinit so that we can later initialize it in onCreate. It will then be canceled in onDestroy.

```
1   override fun onCreate(savedInstanceState: Bundle?) {
2       super.onCreate(savedInstanceState)
3       job = Job()
4       ...
5   }
6
7   override fun onDestroy() {
8       job.cancel()
9       super.onDestroy()
10  }
```

So now, code gets simpler when using coroutines. You can just use the builder and skip the coroutine context, as it will use the one defined by the scope, which includes the main dispatcher:

```
1   launch {
2       ...
3   }
```

Of course, if you're using coroutines on all your activities, it may be worth extracting that code to a parent class.

Extra - Convert callbacks to coroutines

If you've started thinking of using coroutines in your project, you're probably wondering how you're going to keep your current libraries, which may be making use of callbacks, into your new shiny coroutines.

The thing is that the maintainers probably haven't given support to coroutines yet, so mixing coroutines with callbacks may be a bit awful. Luckily, there's an easy way to do it.

Imagine that your library provides a function called doLoginAsync(), which receives a callback as a second argument. The coroutines library provides a function called suspendCancellableCoroutine that will help you do the job:

```
1   suspend fun suspendAsyncLogin(username: String, password: String): User =
2       suspendCancellableCoroutine { continuation ->
3           userService.doLoginAsync(username, password) { user ->
4               continuation.resume(user)
5           }
6       }
```

This function returns a continuation object that can be used to return the result of the callback. Just call continuation.resume, and that result will be returned by the suspending function to the parent coroutine. It's that easy!

Coroutines open up a world of possibilities and simplify executing background tasks in a way that you probably couldn't imagine.

I really recommend you to start using them in your projects. So let's see how to apply it to our current one.

27.3 Using coroutines in our example

With these concepts already clear, let's modify our example to start using lambdas. We are replacing the usage of doAsync in both activities with a coroutine.

Add the required dependency:

app/build.gradle

```
1   implementation 'org.jetbrains.kotlinx:kotlinx-coroutines-android:1.1.0'
```

To do that, first you need to create a scope. To reuse the configuration, create a parent class that deals with the scope, this way:

activities/CoroutineScopeActivity

```
1   abstract class CoroutineScopeActivity : AppCompatActivity(), CoroutineScope {
2
3       override val coroutineContext: CoroutineContext
4           get() = Dispatchers.Main + job
5
6       lateinit var job: Job
7
8       override fun onCreate(savedInstanceState: Bundle?) {
9           super.onCreate(savedInstanceState)
10          job = Job()
11      }
12
13      override fun onDestroy() {
14          job.cancel()
15          super.onDestroy()
16      }
17  }
```

Then make the activities extend this new abstract one:

activities/MainActivity

```
1   class MainActivity : CoroutineScopeActivity(), ToolbarManager {
2       ...
3   }
```

With that, we can now use the coroutine builders as we saw in the section above:

activities/MainActivity

```
1  private fun loadForecast() = launch {
2      val result = withContext(Dispatchers.IO) { RequestForecastCommand(zipCode).execute() }
3      val adapter = ForecastListAdapter(result) { ... }
4      forecastList.adapter = adapter
5      toolbarTitle = "${result.city} (${result.country})"
6  }
```

As you see, the RequestForecastCommand, which is executed in a background thread by Dispatchers.IO, returns the result that can then be used by the following lines.

You can even simplify this a bit more if you convert execute() to a suspending function:

domain/commands/Command

```
1  interface Command<out T> {
2      suspend fun execute(): T
3  }
```

domain/commands/RequestForecastCommand

```
1  override suspend fun execute() = withContext(Dispatchers.IO) {
2      forecastProvider.requestByZipCode(zipCode, DAYS)
3  }
```

That prevents from requiring to write withContext inside the coroutine, and forces to use this command in a worker thread:

activities/MainActivity

```
1  private fun loadForecast() = launch {
2      val result = RequestForecastCommand(zipCode).execute()
3      val adapter = ForecastListAdapter(result) { ... }
4      ...
5  }
```

You can do the same with the DetailActivity:

domain/commands/RequestDayForecastCommand

```
1   override suspend fun execute() = withContext(Dispatchers.IO) {
2       forecastProvider.requestForecast(id)
3   }
```

activities/DetailActivity

```
1   launch {
2       val id = intent.getLongExtra(ID, -1)
3       val result = RequestDayForecastCommand(id).execute()
4       bindForecast(result)
5   }
```

So with all this, you now have your asynchronous code written synchronously very easily. As I said at the beginning, this code is quite simple, but imagine convoluted cases where the result of one background operation is used by the next one, or when you need to iterate over a list and execute a request per item. All this can be written as regular synchronous code, which is much easier to read and maintain.

Bye bye, callback hell. Check new changes in chapter-27[55] branch.

---

[55]https://github.com/antoniolg/Kotlin-for-Android-Developers/tree/chapter-27

28 Testing your App

We are reaching the end of this trip. You already learned most Kotlin features throughout this book, but you are probably wondering if you can test your Android Apps using Kotlin exclusively. The answer is: of course!

In Android, we have a couple of different tests: unit and instrumentation tests. This book is not meant to teach you how to write tests; there are entire books dedicated to that matter. My goal in this chapter is to explain how to prepare your environment to be able to write some tests and show you that Kotlin also works fine for testing.

28.1 Unit testing

I will not get into discussions about what unit testing means. There are many definitions out there with some slight differences. A general idea could be that unit tests are the tests that validate an individual unit of source code. What a 'unit' involves is left to the reader. For the sake of simplicity, I am defining a unit test as a test that does not need a device to run. The IDE can run the tests and show a result that identifies which tests succeeded and which ones failed.

Unit testing is usually done using the JUnit library. So let's add the dependency to the build.gradle. As this dependency is only used when running tests, we can use testImplementation instead of implementation. This way, the library is left out for regular compilations, reducing the size of the APK:

app/build.gradle

```
1  dependencies {
2      ...
3      testImplementation "junit:junit:4.12"
4  }
```

Now sync Gradle to get the library included in your project. In old versions of Android Studio, you may need to choose which kind of tests you want to run. Go to the 'Build Variants' tab (you probably have it on the left side of the IDE) and click on 'Test Artifact' dropdown. You should choose 'Unit Tests' there. New Android Studio versions can have both kinds of tests enabled at the same time, so this step is not required.

Another thing you need to do is create a new folder. Below src, you already probably have androidTest and main. Create another one called test, and a folder called java below. So now you should have a src/test/java folder colored in green. This is a good indication that the IDE detected that we are in 'Unit Test' mode and that this folder contains test files.

Let's write a simple test to check everything works properly. Create a new Kotlin class called SimpleTest using the proper package (*com.antonioleiva.weatherapp* in my case, but you need to use the main package of your app). Once you have created the new file, write this simple test:

test/SimpleTest.kt

```
1   import org.junit.Test
2   import kotlin.test.assertTrue
3
4   class SimpleTest {
5       @Test
6       fun `unit testing works`() {
7           assertTrue(true)
8       }
9   }
```

Use the @Test annotation to identify the function as a test. Be sure to use org.unit.Test. Then add a simple assertion. It only checks that true is true, which should succeed.

Did you see how I wrote the name of the function? If you use backquotes, you can provide a readable name for your tests. When tests run in Android Studio, the summary shows texts that are much easier to read.

You will see that these names show an error. It is because this format is not available for Android code, so it is not available for instrumentation tests. But you can use them without issues in unit tests, so you can disable the inspection just for tests and use it safely.

To execute the tests, right click on the new `java` folder you created below `test`, and choose 'Run All Tests'. When the compilation finishes, it will run the test, and you will see a summary showing the result. You should notice that your test passed.

Now it is time to create some real tests. Everything that deals with the Android framework probably needs an instrumentation test or some extra libraries such as Robolectric[56]. Because of that, in these examples, I am testing things that do not use anything from the framework. For instance, I will test the extension function that creates a date `String` from a `Long`.

Create a new file called `ExtensionTests`, and add this tests:

test/ExtensionsTest.kt

```
1  class ExtensionsTest {
2      @Test
3      fun `"longToDateString" returns valid value`() {
4          assertEquals("Oct 19, 2015", 1445275635000L.toDateString())
5      }
6
7      @Test
8      fun `"longToDateString" with full format returns valid value`() {
9          assertEquals("Monday, October 19, 2015",
10             1445275635000L.toDateString(DateFormat.FULL))
11     }
12 }
```

These tests check that a `Long` instance is properly converted to a `String`. The first one tests the default behavior (which uses `DateFormat.MEDIUM`), while the second one specifies a different format. Run the tests and see that all of them pass. I also recommend you to change something and see how it crashes.

If you are used to testing your apps in Java, you will see there is not much difference here. I have covered a simple example, but from here you can create more complex tests to validate other parts of the app. For instance, we could write some tests for `ForecastProvider`. We can use `Mockito` library to mock some other classes and be able to test the provider independently:

---

[56]http://robolectric.org/

build.gradle

```
1   buildscript {
2       . . .
3       ext.mockito_version = '2.23.4'
4   }
```

app/build.gradle

```
1   dependencies {
2       . . .
3       testImplementation "junit:junit:4.12"
4       testImplementation "org.mockito:mockito-core:$mockito_version"
5   }
```

Now create a ForecastProviderTest. We are going to test that a ForecastProvider with a DataSource that returns something will get a result that is not null. So first we need to mock a ForecastDataSource:

test/domain/datasource/ForecastProviderTest.kt

```
1   val ds = mock(ForecastDataSource::class.java)
2   `when`(ds.requestDayForecast(0)).then {
3       Forecast(0, 0, "desc", 20, 0, "url")
4   }
```

As you see, we need backquotes for when function, because when is a reserved word in Kotlin. So we need to escape it if we find some Java code that uses it.

An alternative would be to rename the import:

```
1   import org.mockito.Mockito.`when` as whenever
2
3   . . .
4
5   whenever(ds.requestDayForecast(0)).then { ... }
```

It is up to you; I will use the backquotes in this case.

Now we create a provider with this data source, and check that the result of the call to that method is not null:

```
1   val provider = ForecastProvider(listOf(ds))
2   assertNotNull(provider.requestForecast(0))
```

This is the complete test function:

test/domain/datasource/ForecastProviderTest.kt

```
1   @Test fun `data source returns a value`() {
2       val ds = mock(ForecastDataSource::class.java)
3       `when`(ds.requestDayForecast(0)).then {
4           Forecast(0, 0, "desc", 20, 0, "url")
5       }
6
7       val provider = ForecastProvider(listOf(ds))
8       assertNotNull(provider.requestForecast(0))
9   }
```

If you run this, you will see that it crashes. Thanks to this test, we are detecting we have something wrong in our code. The test is failing because ForecastProvider is initializing SOURCES inside its companion object before it is used. We can add some sources to the ForecastProvider through the constructor, and this static list would never be used, so it should be lazy loaded:

domain/datasource/ForecastProvider.kt

```
1   companion object {
2       val DAY_IN_MILLIS = 1000 * 60 * 60 * 24
3       val SOURCES by lazy { listOf(ForecastDb(), ForecastServer()) }
4   }
```

If you now run again, you will see it is now passing all the tests.

We can also test, for instance, that when a source returns null, it will iterate over the next source to get a result:

test/domain/datasource/ForecastProviderTest.kt

```
1   @Test fun `empty database returns server value`() {
2       val db = mock(ForecastDataSource::class.java)
3
4       val server = mock(ForecastDataSource::class.java)
5       `when`(server.requestForecastByZipCode(
6               any(Long::class.java), any(Long::class.java)))
7               .then {
8                   ForecastList(0, "city", "country", listOf())
9               }
10
11      val provider = ForecastProvider(listOf(db, server))
12
13      assertNotNull(provider.requestByZipCode(0, 0))
14  }
```

As you see, the simple dependency inversion we solved by using default values for arguments is enough to let us implement some simple unit tests. There are many more things we could test about this provider, but this example is enough to show that we can use the basic unit testing tools.

28.2 Mocking closed classes

In Kotlin, everything is closed by default, so you may find yourself in trouble when you want to mock a class. Mockito cannot mock closed (final) classes.

So imagine we want to test RequestDayForecastCommand, and check that when its execute() method is called, the provider is also called. We could do this:

test/domain/commands/RequestDayForecastCommandTest.kt

```
1   class RequestDayForecastCommandTest {
2
3       @Test
4       fun `provider is called when command is executed`() {
5           val forecastProvider = mock(ForecastProvider::class.java)
6           val command = RequestDayForecastCommand(2, forecastProvider)
7
8           runBlocking { command.execute() }
9
10          verify(forecastProvider).requestForecast(2)
11      }
12  }
```

Remember that as command.execute() is a suspending function, it must be called in a coroutine context. Here's where the runBlocking builder comes in very handy.

But if you run this test, you will find that it fails:

```
1   Mockito cannot mock/spy because :
2    - final class
```

You have two options to overcome this situation:

- Use the open reserved word, which would allow Mockito to mock your class, but also any other class to extend this one (which was probably closed for a reason).
- Extract an interface, and mock the interface. This one is a cleaner solution, but also slightly redundant if you are not using that interface for anything else.

There is, however, a third alternative: an experimental feature in Mockito 2. This feature allows you to mock final classes and avoid those extra artifacts. It might be that by the time you read these lines, the feature is not experimental anymore. But if it still is, you need to add an extra library to opt in for the feature:

app/build.gradle

```
1  testImplementation "org.mockito:mockito-inline:$mockito_version"
```

Even if it is experimental, it works pretty well, so feel safe to use it.

Now you can rerun your test, and see how it magically passes.

28.3 Instrumentation tests

Instrumentation tests are a bit different. They are typically used to test UI interactions, where we need an Application instance to be running by the time the tests are executed. To do this, we need to deploy the app and run the tests on a device.

This type of tests reside in the androidTest folder, and we must change 'Test Artifact' to 'Android Instrumentation Tests' in 'Build Variants' panel on old Android Studio versions. The official library to implement instrumentation tests is Espresso[57], which helps us easily navigate through our App by writing Actions, and filter and check results using ViewMatchers and Matchers.

The configuration is a bit harder than the previous one. We need a bunch of extra libraries and Gradle configuration. The good thing is that Kotlin does not add any extra overhead, so if you already know how to configure Espresso, it should be easy for you.

First, specify the test runner in defaultConfig:

app/build.gradle

```
1  defaultConfig {
2      ...
3      testInstrumentationRunner "android.support.test.runner.AndroidJUnitRunner"
4  }
```

Once you have configured the runner, it is time to add the rest of the dependencies, this time using androidTestImplementation. That way, these libraries are only added when we compile to run the instrumentation tests:

---

[57]https://google.github.io/android-testing-support-library/

build.gradle

```
1   buildscript {
2       . . .
3       ext.test_support_version = '1.0.2'
4       ext.espresso_version = '3.0.2'
5   }
```

{title="app/build.gradle", lang="groovy"}f dependencies { ... androidTestImplementation "com.android.support:support-annotations:$support_version" androidTestImplementation "com.android.support.test:runner:$test_support_version" androidTestImplementation "com.android.support.test:rules:$test_support_version" androidTestImplementation "com.android.support.test.espresso:espresso-core:$espresso_version" androidTestImplementation("com.android.support.test.espresso:espresso-contrib:$espresso_version") { exclude group: 'com.android.support', module: 'appcompat-v7' exclude group: 'com.android.support', module: 'support-v4' exclude group: 'com.android.support', module: 'design' exclude group: 'com.android.support', module: 'recyclerview-v7' }

I do not want to spend much time talking about this, but here it is a brief explanation of why you need these libraries:

- runner: It is the test runner, the one we specified in defaultConfig.
- rules: Includes some rules that help tests inflate and launch the activities. We will use a rule in our examples.
- espresso-core: the basic features of Espresso, the library that makes instrument tests easier.
- espresso-contrib: it adds some extra features, such as RecyclerView testing support. We have to exclude some of its dependencies, because we already have them in the project, and tests crash otherwise.

Let's now create a simple example. The test will click on the first row of the forecast list, and check that it can find a view with the id R.id.weatherDescription. This view is in the DetailActivity, which implies that we successfully navigated to the detail after clicking on a view inside the RecyclerView.

```
1   class SimpleInstrumentationTest {
2
3       @get:Rule
4       val activityRule = ActivityTestRule(MainActivity::class.java)
5
6       ...
7   }
```

We need to create an activity rule, which instantiates the activity that the test will use. In Java, you would annotate the field using @Rule. However, as you know, fields and properties are not the same, so if you use just that, the execution will fail because the access to the field inside the property is not public. What you need to do is to annotate the getter. Kotlin allows doing that by specifying get or set before the name of the rule. In this case, write @get:Rule.

After that, we are ready to create our first test:

```
1   @Test fun itemClickNavigatesToDetail() {
2       onView(withId(R.id.forecastList)).perform(
3               RecyclerViewActions
4                   .actionOnItemAtPosition<RecyclerView.ViewHolder>(0, click()))
5       onView(withId(R.id.weatherDescription))
6               .check(matches(isAssignableFrom(TextView::class.java)))
7   }
```

As these tests run on a device, we cannot use the same naming format we used for unit tests. Otherwise, it will crash.

The function is annotated with @Test, the same way we did with unit tests. We can start using Espresso in the body of the test. It first performs a click over the first position of the recycler. Then, it checks that it can find a view with a specific id and that it is an instance of TextView.

To run the test, you can do the same you did for unit tests: right click on the java folder below androidTest, and choose 'Run All Tests'. Now, in 'Target device', choose the target you prefer. Click 'OK' and then run. You should see how the app starts on your device, and the test clicks on the first position, opens the detail activity and closes the App again.

Now we are going to do a more difficult one. The test will open the overflow from the Toolbar, click on Settings action, change the city code and check that the Toolbar title has changed to the corresponding one.

```
1   @Test fun modifyZipCodeChangesToolbarTitle() {
2       openActionBarOverflowOrOptionsMenu(activityRule.activity)
3       onView(withText(R.string.settings)).perform(click())
4       onView(withId(R.id.cityCode)).perform(replaceText("94301"))
5       pressBack()
6       onView(isAssignableFrom(Toolbar::class.java))
7           .check(matches(
8               withToolbarTitle(`is`("Palo Alto (US)"))))
9   }
```

What the test exactly does is:

- It first opens the overflow by using openActionBarOverflowOrOptionsMenu.
- It then finds a view with the Settings text and performs a click on it.
- After that, the settings activity opens, so it looks for the EditText and replaces the old city code with a new one.
- It presses the back button, which saves the new value in the preferences, and closes the activity.
- As onResume is executed in MainActivity, the request is performed again. This retrieves the forecast of the new city.
- The last line checks the Toolbar title and sees whether it matches with the proper value.

There is not a default matcher to check Toolbar title, but Espresso is easy to extend, so we can create a new matcher which implements the check:

```
1   private fun withToolbarTitle(textMatcher: Matcher<CharSequence>): Matcher<Any> =
2           object : BoundedMatcher<Any, Toolbar>(Toolbar::class.java) {
3
4               override fun matchesSafely(toolbar: Toolbar): Boolean =
5                   textMatcher.matches(toolbar.title)
6
7               override fun describeTo(description: Description) {
8                   description.appendText("with toolbar title: ")
9                   textMatcher.describeTo(description)
10              }
11          }
```

The `matchesSafely` function is the place where the check happens, while the `describeTo` function adds some information about the matcher.

This chapter has been especially interesting because we have seen how Kotlin is entirely compatible with both unit and integration tests and can interoperate with the testing libraries. Take a look at the code[58] and run the tests by yourself.

---

[58]https://github.com/antoniolg/Kotlin-for-Android-Developers/tree/chapter-28

29 Extra concepts

Throughout this book, we have talked about the most important concepts of the Kotlin language. But we did not use some of them when implementing the app, and I would not want to let them out of these pages. In this chapter, I will review some unrelated features that you could be helpful for you when you develop your next Android app using Kotlin.

29.1 Nested classes

As in Java, we can define classes inside other classes. By default, an inner class will not be able to access the members of the outer class (it would behave as a static class in Java):

```
1   class Outer {
2     private val bar: Int = 1
3     class Nested {
4       fun foo() = 2
5     }
6   }
7
8   val demo = Outer.Nested().foo() // == 2
```

This is what we used for instance for the ViewHolder inside the ForecastListAdapter. If we want to access to the members of the outer class, we need to declare it as an **inner** class:

```
1   class Outer {
2     private val bar: Int = 1
3     inner class Inner {
4       fun foo() = bar
5     }
6   }
7
8   val demo = Outer().Inner().foo() // === 1
```

29.2 Enum classes

Kotlin also provides a way to implement enum:

```
1   enum class Day {
2       SUNDAY, MONDAY, TUESDAY, WEDNESDAY,
3       THURSDAY, FRIDAY, SATURDAY
4   }
```

Enums can have parameters, which are declared in the constructor:

```
1   enum class Icon(val res: Int) {
2       UP(R.drawable.ic_up),
3       SEARCH(R.drawable.ic_search),
4       CAST(R.drawable.ic_cast)
5   }
6
7   val searchIconRes = Icon.SEARCH.res
```

Enums can be requested by the String that matches the name, and we can also get an Array that includes all the values of an Enum, so that we can iterate over them.

```
1   val search: Icon = Icon.valueOf("SEARCH")
2   val iconList: Array<Icon> = Icon.values
```

Besides, each Enum constant has functions to obtain its name and the position in the declaration:

```
1  val searchName: String = Icon.SEARCH.name
2  val searchPosition: Int = Icon.SEARCH.ordinal
```

Enums implement `Comparable` based on the ordinal, so it is easy to compare them.

29.3 Sealed classes

Sealed classes are used to represent restricted class hierarchies, which means that the number of classes that extend a sealed class is restricted. It is similar to an Enum in the sense that the compiler is aware of the number of subtypes a sealed class has. The difference is that enum instances are unique, while sealed classes can have multiple instances which can contain different states.

We could implement, for instance, something similar to the `Option` class: a type that prevents the use of `null` by returning a `Some` class when the object contains a value or the `None` instance when it is empty:

```
1  sealed class Option<out T>
2  object None : Option<Nothing>()
3  data class Just<out T>(val value: T) : Option<T>()
```

The good thing about sealed classes is that when they are used in a `when` expression, we can check all the options and will not need to add the `else` clause. Also, if at some point we add a new subclass, the compiler will warn us about the places where we should be dealing with it.

```
1  val result = when (option) {
2      None -> "Empty"
3      is Just -> "Contains a value"
4  }
```

29.4 Exceptions

In Kotlin, all exceptions implement `Throwable`, have a message and are unchecked. Consequently, we are not required to use `try/catch` on any of them. That is not the case in Java, where methods that throw IOException, for instance, need to be surrounded by a try/catch block. Time has shown that checked exceptions were not a good idea. People like Bruce Eckel[59], Rod Waldhoff[60] or Anders Hejlsberg[61] can give you a better perspective on it.

The way to throw an exception is very similar to Java:

```
1   throw MyException("Exception message")
```

And try expression is identical too:

```
1   try {
2     // some code
3   }
4   catch (e: SomeException) {
5     // handler
6   }
7   finally {
8     // optional finally block
9   }
```

Both throw and try are expressions in Kotlin, which allows to assign them to a variable. This is useful when dealing with edge cases:

```
1   val s = when(x){
2       is Int -> "Int instance"
3       is String -> "String instance"
4       else -> throw UnsupportedOperationException("Not valid type")
5   }
```

or

```
1   val s = try { x as String } catch(e: ClassCastException) { null }
```

---

[59]http://www.mindview.net/Etc/Discussions/CheckedExceptions
[60]http://radio-weblogs.com/0122027/stories/2003/04/01/JavasCheckedExceptionsWereAMistake.html
[61]http://www.artima.com/intv/handcuffs.html

30 Java interoperability

So far, we have been talking about creating an app from scratch. However, you probably find yourself in a situation where you already have an App written in Java with thousands of lines of code, and you cannot convert all your code. I will cover this topic here.

One of the great wonders of Kotlin is that it is entirely interoperable with Java. Therefore, although all your application code is written Java, you can create a class in Kotlin and use it from Java without any issues. Calling Kotlin from Java code cannot be easier. This potentially gives you two advantages:

- You can use Kotlin in a Java project: In any project, you have already started, you can decide to start writing new code in Kotlin. You can then call it from Java code.
- If you do not know how to do something in Kotlin, you can write that part in Java. You may be wondering if there is a case where Kotlin is not enough to do something on Android. In theory, everything can be done, but the fact is that it does not matter. If you cannot do it in Kotlin, then implement that part in Java.

Let's see how this compatibility works, and how Kotlin code looks when used from Java.

30.1 Package-level functions

In Kotlin, functions do not need to be inside a class, but this is not the case in Java. How can we call a function then? Imagine that we have a file called utils.kt that looks like this:

```
1   fun logD(message: String) {
2       Log.d("", message)
3   }
4
5   fun logE(message: String) {
6       Log.e("", message)
7   }
```

In Java we can access them through a class that will be called UtilsKt, with some static methods:

```
1   UtilsKt.logD("Debug");
2   UtilsKt.logE("Error");
```

30.2 Extension functions

We have been using extension functions a lot throughout this book. However, how do they look in Java? If you have the following function:

```
1   fun ViewGroup.inflate(resId: Int, attachToRoot: Boolean = false): View {
2       return LayoutInflater.from(context).inflate(resId, this, attachToRoot)
3   }
```

This is applied to a ViewGroup. It receives a layout and inflates it using the parent view. What would we get if we want to use it in Java? This is the result:

```
1   View v = UtilsKt.inflate(parent, R.layout.view_item, false);
```

As you can see, the object that applies this function (the receiver) is added as an argument to the function. Besides, the optional argument becomes mandatory, because in Java we cannot use default values.

30.3 Function overloads

If you want to generate the corresponding overloads in Java, you can use @JvmOver-loads annotation for that function. In the previous example, you would not need to specify false for the second argument in Java:

```
1   @JvmOverloads
2   fun ViewGroup.inflate(resId: Int, attachToRoot: Boolean = false): View {
3       return LayoutInflater.from(context).inflate(resId, this, attachToRoot)
4   }
5
6   View v = UtilsKt.inflate(parent, R.layout.view_item);
```

If you prefer to specify the name of the class when calling Kotlin from Java, you can use an annotation to modify it. In the utils.kt file, add this above the package sentence:

```
1   @file:JvmName("AndroidUtils")
```

And now the class in Java will be named:

```
1   AndroidUtils.logD("Debug");
2   AndroidUtils.logE("Error");
3   View v = AndroidUtils.inflate(parent, R.layout.view_item, false);
```

30.4 Instance and static fields

In Java, we use fields to store the state. They can be instance fields, which means that each object can store a different value, or static (all instances of a class share them). If we try to find an equivalent of this in Kotlin, it would be properties and companion objects. If we have a class like this:

```
1   class App : Application() {
2
3       val appHelper = AppHelper()
4
5       companion object {
6           lateinit var instance: App
7       }
8
9       override fun onCreate() {
10          super.onCreate()
11          instance = this
12      }
13
14  }
```

How does this work in Java? You can simply access the companion object properties as static fields, by using getters and setters:

```
1   AppHelper helper = App.instance.getAppHelper();
```

As a val, it only generates the getter in Java. If it were var, we would also have a setter. The access to instance has worked automatically because it uses the lateinit annotation, which also exposes the field that Kotlin uses to store the state. But imagine we create a constant:

```
1   companion object {
2       lateinit var instance: App
3       val CONSTANT = 27
4   }
```

You find that you cannot use it directly. You are forced to access through a Companion internal class:

```
1   KotlinClass.Companion.getCONSTANT()
```

This previous snippet does not look particularly readable. To expose the field in Java the same way a static field would look, you need a new annotation:

```
1   @JvmField val CONSTANT = 27
```

And now you can use it from Java code:

```
1   int c = App.CONSTANT;
```

If you have functions in a companion object, they are converted to static methods using the @JvmStatic annotation. There are several ways to define constants that, when we use Kotlin from Java, generate different bytecode. If you remember, we used const val before, and those properties are accessible without using a getter.

30.5 Data classes

Some features are clear, but some others are more difficult to know how they may behave in Java. So let's take a look at those features that Kotlin has, but Java does not. One example is *data classes*. Let's say we have a data class like this:

```
1   data class MediaItem(val id: Int, val title: String, val url: String)
```

We can create instances of this class:

```
1   MediaItem mediaItem = new MediaItem(1, "Title", "https://antonioleiva.com");
```

But are we missing something? First, let's check if `equals` works as expected:

```
1   MediaItem mediaItem = new MediaItem(1, "Title", "https://antonioleiva.com");
2   MediaItem mediaItem2 = new MediaItem(1, "Title", "https://antonioleiva.com");
3
4   if (mediaItem.equals(mediaItem2)) {
5       Toast.makeText(this, "Items are equals", Toast.LENGTH_SHORT).show();
6   }
```

Of course, it shows the Toast. The bytecode the class generates has everything it needs to compare two items and, if the state is the same, then the items are also the same. However, other things are more difficult to replicate. Remember the copy feature data classes have? The method is there, but you can only use it passing all arguments:

```
1   mediaItem.copy(1, "Title2", "http://google.com");
```

So it is not better than just using the constructor. Also, we lose destructuring, as the Java language does not have a way to express that.

30.6 Sealed classes

Another feature that may come to your mind is *sealed classes*. How do they work when used from Java? Let's try it:

```
1   sealed class Filter {
2       object None : Filter()
3       data class ByType(val type: Type) : Filter()
4       data class ByFormat(val format: Format) : Filter()
5   }
```

We have a Filter class that represents a filter that can be applied to items. Of course, in Java we cannot do:

```
1   public void filter(Filter filter) {
2       switch (filter) {
3           ...
4       }
5   }
```

switch in Java only accepts a small number of types, and for Java, sealed classes are regular classes. So the best you can do is:

```
1   if (filter instanceof Filter.None) {
2       Log.d(TAG, "Nothing to filter");
3   } else if (filter instanceof Filter.ByType) {
4       Filter.ByType type = (Filter.ByType) filter;
5       Log.d(TAG, "Type is: " + type.getType().toString());
6   } else if (filter instanceof Filter.ByFormat) {
7       Filter.ByFormat format = ((Filter.ByFormat) filter);
8       Log.d(TAG, "Format is: " + format.getFormat());
9   }
```

We cannot make use of any of the extra features from Java.

30.7 Inline functions and reified types

As you may remember, in Kotlin you can make generic functions use reified types. That way, you can use the generic type inside the function.

When we saw them, I mentioned that they need to use the reserved word inline, which is used to substitute the calls to the function by the body of the function when compiling. Can we use that from Java?

Let's start with the inline functions, which are easier to test. If we have a toast function that receives the message as a lambda:

```
1    inline fun Context.toast(message: () -> CharSequence) {
2        Toast.makeText(this, message(), Toast.LENGTH_SHORT).show()
3    }
```

We can use it without issues like this from Java:

```
1    ExtensionsKt.toast(this, () -> "Hello World");
```

So inline functions work, but there is an interesting thing here. When used from Kotlin, the decompiled code looks like this:

```
1    Toast.makeText(this, "Hello", 0).show();
```

The function is being inlined as expected. What happens when used from Java?

```
1    ExtensionsKt.toast(this, DetailActivity$$Lambda$0.$instance);
```

So, though you can use `inline` functions from Java, they are actually not inlined. It is calling the function and creating an object for the lambda. That is something to take into account.

Now, what happens to reified types? This is a function that navigates to the activity specified in the generic type:

```
1    inline fun <reified T : Activity> Context.startActivity() {
2        startActivity(Intent(this, T::class.java))
3    }
```

Then, if you try to call this function from Java, you will see that this method appears to be private, so we cannot use it. Reified functions are not are not available from Java code.

So now you understand better how all new Kotlin features behave when used from Java. You see that using the code we write in Kotlin from Java is effortless. Most of them can still be used, though certainly, we cannot take advantage of some Kotlin features from Java.

31 Conclusion

Thanks for reading this book. Throughout this pages, we have learned Kotlin by implementing an Android app as an example. The weather app was an excellent example to play with the essential features most apps need: a master/detail UI, communication with an API, database storage, shared preferences...

The good thing about this method is that you have learned the most important Kotlin concepts while using them. In my opinion, it is easier to absorb new knowledge when you put it into action. It was my primary goal, because reference books are usually a helpful tool to solve some specific doubts, but they are hard to read from the beginning to the very end. Besides, as the examples are usually out of context, it is difficult to understand which kind of problems those features solve.

That was, in fact, the other goal of the book: to show you real problems we face in Android and how they can be solved using Kotlin. Any Android developer struggles with many questions when dealing with asynchrony, databases, or has to implement verbose listeners or activity navigations. By using a real app as an example, we have answered many of these questions while learning the new language features.

I hope I achieved these goals, and I wish that you not only learned Kotlin but also enjoyed reading this book. Now that Google has adopted Kotlin, I am convinced that learning the language is the way to go: you will enjoy developing apps and get prepared for this new skill that is becoming a need in many Android job positions these days.

This book is finished, but it does not mean that it is dead. I will keep updating it to the latest versions of Kotlin, reviewing and improving it based on your comments and suggestions. Feel free to write me about it at any moment and tell me what you think, the errors you find, concepts that are not clear enough or whatever concern you may have.

It has been a fantastic journey during the months I have been writing this book. I have learned a lot too, so thanks again for helping 'Kotlin for Android Developers' to become a reality.

Best,

Antonio Leiva

- Site: antonioleiva.com[62]
- Email: contact@antonioleiva.com[63]
- Twitter: @lime_cl[64]
- Google+: +AntonioLeivaGordillo[65]

---

[62]http://antonioleiva.com
[63]mailto:contact@antonioleiva.com
[64]http://twitter.com/lime_cl
[65]http://plus.google.com/+AntonioLeivaGordillo